Contents

Foreword

From the Archbishop of Canterbury

From earliest times Christians have faced many issues raised by their relationships with people of other faiths. These can range from questions about the practicalities of daily life alongside people of other faith communities to the deepest of theological reflections about the nature of the God we worship. What we certainly cannot do, therefore, is dismiss Christian reflection on such matters as a somewhat exotic activity on the fringes of the Church's proper agenda. Rather, there is a pressing need, especially where Christians are in regular contact with friends, neighbours or colleagues of other faiths, for resources that will help us think and pray more deeply, in the light of Scripture and our theological traditions, about the challenges and the opportunities presented to us by inter faith relationships.

So I warmly welcome the publication of *Faith Meeting Faith* by the Methodist Church. In a comparatively short space it identifies and explores a comprehensive list of questions, in ways that should prove extremely useful both for the individual reader and for groups. An impressive feature is the sensitivity and intelligence with which the diversity of views among Christians about some key issues is acknowledged. All Christians should find that their views and concerns are taken seriously here; equally, all should find that they are challenged to think afresh.

As we live out the implications of the Covenant between the Church of England and the Methodist Church in Great Britain, signed in 2003, it is a particular pleasure for me to commend *Faith Meeting Faith*. This book has grown out of the commitment and expertise of those working in inter faith relationships in the Methodist Church, often in partnership with Anglicans and members of other Christian churches. They have provided a valuable resource for us all, and I hope that Christians of many traditions will make good use of it.

+Rowan Cantuar:

Introduction

Have you...

- met people of other faiths in public places such as the post office, the bank, the doctor's, your local newsagent, a hospital, a school or college,
or had someone of another faith move into your street?

- passed a place of worship – mosque, gurdwara, Hindu temple – and wondered what it was like inside?

- worked alongside someone of another faith
or heard people of other faiths speaking about what faith means to them?

- seen a programme about another faith on television
or been surprised by how a newspaper has portrayed another faith?

- wondered whether religion really endorses violence
or asked whether political parties that stress the danger of asylum seekers are right?

- visited a country where Christians are a minority alongside other faiths
or had contact with someone who lives in a country where another faith is in the majority?

- stayed in a guesthouse or hostel where people of another faith were also staying?

- had a friend or relative marry someone of another faith
or seen them convert to another faith?

- been aware of neighbours celebrating a religious festival?

- welcomed asylum seekers of other faiths into your community?

- wondered what to say about your own faith to a person of another faith
or feared that the presence of different faiths in Britain may threaten social harmony?

If you have said yes to any of these, this resource will interest you. The 2001 census showed that Britain is home to more than three million people of faiths other than Christianity. Some belong to long-established communities. Others have come more recently as asylum seekers or refugees. Few people in Britain are untouched by the presence of other faiths in today's society. Some see it as a gift that will make our societies spiritually stronger. Some greet it with apprehension, fearing it will fuel social division or threaten the "Christian" character of our land. Others simply don't know what to think.

But think we must if we are to live effectively as Christians in a religiously diverse Britain. One task is to learn about what people of other faiths believe and practise. Another is to reflect on questions about presence and engagement. How are we, as Christians, to be fully "present" in our society, aware of what is around us, sharing what we believe and putting what we believe into action? And how do we "engage" with our neighbours of other faiths and with the questions that they are asking of us?

This resource is written by Christians for Christians, to help tackle this second task. It takes 30 questions that Christians ask about inter-faith relations and explores:

- Why is the question asked?

- What responses do people make?

- What should we consider when making our own response?

- Ways forward.

The material does not give all the answers, nor does it present one, unified theology of inter-faith relations. Its aim is to provoke thought, discussion and action, recognising that Christians come to inter-faith relations with different experiences and different approaches. It complements material about what people of other faiths believe and practise (see the Resources section on pages 68-70, and "Supplementary material" on page 7).

Woven into the material is an affirmation of four kinds of inter-faith dialogue or encounter, which were first identified in 1984 by the Roman Catholic Church:

- dialogue of life – a living together in friendship;

- dialogue of joint social action – a working together for justice and peace;

- dialogue of the intellect – a coming together to seek clearer understandings of truth through discussion and debate;

- dialogue of religious experience – a sharing of insights from prayer and meditation.

How to use the material

The material is suitable for individual and for group use. Although group leaders may choose to start at the beginning and work through to the end, it is more likely that they will select from the questions, taking the local context and the interests of the group into account. The questions overlap and can be put together in various ways to stimulate discussion. Members of the group should be encouraged to share their views honestly, but with sensitivity and a willingness to listen.

The questions deal with five related areas: mission; the practical dynamics of dialogue; socio-economic questions; scripture; theology. It is hoped that none of these is avoided when questions to study are chosen. For each of these areas is important.

The exploration of each question invites various forms of reflection/discussion:

Why is the question asked? (the introductory text in blue type)
Is this an important question for you? If so, why?

Ways in which people may respond to the question
Which response listed, if any, do you identify with and why?
Can you think of any other responses?

Points to consider
Do any points surprise you? If so, why?
Do any points help you? If so, why?
Do you disagree with any of the points? If so, why?
Do any points anger you? If so, why?
Would you want to add any other points to consider?
Do you need any more information to understand the points being made?

Ways forward
Which way forward appeals to you?
Which would be possible for you?
How will you pursue it?
Can you involve others, for instance the wider church community?
Are there any other ways forward that would be in line with the "Points to consider"?

Supplementary material

Groups or individuals wishing to explore the beliefs and practices of people of other faiths, as a complementary activity to studying *Faith Meeting Faith* are recommended to consider the following. Further details can be found in the Resources section on pages 68-70.

- *The Life We Share: a study pack on inter faith relations*. This contains a CD and a CD rom with the voices of 15 people, from five faiths, speaking about nine life themes. These are accompanied by reflection sheets, Bible studies and worship material. The pack is a joint production between the Methodist Church and USPG, published in 2003.

- *Paths of Faith*: an expanded version of a series of articles on nine faiths and movements, which first appeared in the *Methodist Recorder*. The resource is published by Christians Aware. It includes recommended questions for group discussion.

- *Meeting Buddhists*
  Meeting Hindus } a series of books published by Christians Aware.
  Meeting Sikhs

- The courses run on other faiths by Faith to Faith (see page 68).

Is Britain ceasing to be a Christian country?

This is a common concern. When we look at the major holidays of the year, the ceremonies of our public life, or our landscape dotted with churches, we are reminded of the ways in which Christianity has shaped the past and the present. Yet now it seems that Christianity plays a less central role in people's attitudes than we think it used to. Society is much more secular. At the same time, especially in our towns and cities, religious traditions from around the world are to be found, even flourishing, while some Christian churches struggle to continue.

People may say

- "Christian institutions, such as festivals, schools and church buildings, should have special protection."

- "As a Christian I feel I'm in more of a minority than my parents were."

- "It's more important that Britain is a moral country."

- "There is not less religion; it's just that people express their religious nature in a wider variety of ways."

- "Things haven't changed much where I live."

To consider

Britain has not always been Christian. Christianity was a "foreign import" into Britain in the third and fourth centuries AD, and since then the place of the Church in public and in private life has always been changing. So Christians must ask what they mean when they think of Britain as (once) Christian: patterns of behaviour; a weekly cycle with Sunday kept free; a particular moral code; going to church ...? Which of these do we want to preserve, and why?

> Christians must ask what they mean when they think of Britain as (once) Christian.

Britain's multi-faith experience also goes back further than many realise. There have been British Jews for at least a thousand years. The first Muslims came to Britain at least three hundred years ago – probably earlier. British travellers, explorers and traders, and later soldiers, administrators and members of the Foreign Service, met people of other religious traditions in many parts of the world well before the twentieth century. And students from some of these countries came to study in Britain. Other European countries have an even broader religious past, shown in the long-standing presence of Muslims in the Balkans. If Turkey were to join the European Community, it would bring Islam more firmly into our shared European history.

Perhaps what concerns some people is not so much a question about faith, but that our society has become multi-racial and multi-cultural. The changes in British society over the last 50 years have been considerable and one of the most obvious changes is in this area. It is a change that has enriched many

parts of Britain. Perhaps this change would have taken place even without the presence of other faith traditions.

It is true that the place of the Christian Church in British public life is changing and that many see the Church as no longer taking the lead. However, members of other faith traditions can still see themselves as minorities in a country with a Christian monarchy, a large number of Christian schools and Christmas and Easter as public holidays. And it should not be forgotten that, in the 2001 census, 71.6% of people in the UK declared themselves Christian.

Ways forward

- ☐ **Look for the advantages as well as disadvantages in the changing place and character of religious life in Britain. Look, for example, at how people of other faiths are contributing to the religious life of Britain.**

- ☐ **Witness to God's love in Christ in the world of today.**

- ☐ **Stand up for the values you see as Christian and find others who share them.**

- ☐ **Find out about the history of other faith traditions in Britain.**

Multi-faith, multi-racial, multi-cultural – isn't it all the same?

The presence in Britain of other faiths, other ethnicities and other cultures is often seen as one single factor that has changed British society. Distinctions are not made between the three terms. The result is that sometimes faith is wrongly subsumed into questions of race and culture.

People may say

☐ "Is encountering other faiths just an extension of recognising other cultures, or is it something quite different?"

☐ "Surely the hostility people of some faiths face is simply due to racism?"

☐ "There is still racism in British society and in the Church. Christians must put their own house in order. But I'm not so sure about making friendships with people of other faiths."

☐ "We rejoice in the presence of Christians from many parts of the world in our churches."

☐ "My view is that it's the English culture that's undervalued."

To consider

Some Christians may know of someone in their family or among their friends who has joined another faith tradition, perhaps inspired by the religious convictions of that faith or prompted by friendships or marriage. They will realise that faith, race and culture are categories that need to be distinguished from one another. Each presents Christians with a separate set of questions.

The global Church is *multi-racial*. The Church in Britain has also become increasingly multi-racial as people have moved here, particularly from countries once evangelised from Britain.

Christians have been involved in *multi-faith* encounter in the past when they have travelled abroad, and have had to wrestle with how to understand their experiences. Now that encounter is part of our experience in the UK. This needs to be distinguished from "racial" issues. Faith should not be subsumed into race. There are British Christian people of every ethnic background and colour, and there are British people of other faiths, whatever their colour. Mistrust between faiths in some areas of Britain cannot be addressed through dealing with issues of racial justice alone. It must also be addressed through building faith awareness.

> Mistrust between faiths ... cannot be addressed through dealing with issues of racial justice alone.

In addition, due to heightened opportunities for encounter with other faiths in the last century, there are now a few people who would consider themselves to have multiple or dual religious identity. This is sometimes called "hyphenated identity". For instance, a person might call herself Christian-Hindu or Christian-Buddhist, because she draws from the teachings and practices of both faiths.

Multi-cultural is, perhaps, the most difficult of the three terms, for culture has to do with ethnicity and with faith, but it can be both wider and also more focused than either kinship or faith. Children at school now often learn how Diwali as well as Christmas (Santa Claus and all!) is celebrated. As children in Britain learn about both festivals, perhaps both become part of British culture. But when they learn about them, how much of what they learn is cultural and how much religious? And how are the two related? The so-called British Christmas, for instance, is indebted to a variety of recent and much older traditions, commercial and religious, Christian and non-Christian. Culture and religion are related, but in shifting and asymmetrical ways. After all, there is no single Christian culture. Christianity embraces many cultures.

> Culture and religion are related, but in shifting and asymmetrical ways.

Ways forward

☐ **Look at cultural, racial and religious diversity in the light of our faith in a God who created and loves the world in all its rich variety.**

☐ **Visit another church where many members come from a different ethnic or cultural background from your own.**

☐ **Meet people who share your faith and not your culture, and people who share your culture and not your faith.**

☐ **Look beyond cultural differences to faith when you get to know people of another faith and culture.**

Why should I be interested in other faiths, if there are none near me?

Some Christians live in areas with many opportunities for encountering people of other faiths: at work, among neighbours, among the parents of children at school. Others live in places where there is no synagogue, mosque, gurdwara or Hindu temple. There may be individual families of other faiths, but not communities. In such a situation, it is easy to assume that the lives and beliefs of people of other faiths are simply not relevant.

People may say

"One day I may move, or my children or grandchildren may find friends or partners among people of another faith. I need to be prepared."

"We never know when we may be called 'to give an account of the faith that is in us' to someone of another faith."

"I'm interested, but there are more important local issues to get involved in."

"We're part of a world Church and cannot cut ourselves off from what directly affects other Christians."

"There are no people of other faiths near me, so I haven't time to make it my concern."

To consider

There are very few areas of the UK where there are no people of other faiths. More and more centres providing retreats and education for Buddhists, Muslims and people from other faiths are being situated in rural areas. Community mobility and social change can also pluralise previously mono-cultural neighbourhoods quite rapidly, for instance through the dispersal of asylum seekers. In addition, the media bring people of other faiths into our living rooms. We live in a religiously diverse country and, as global citizens, in a religiously diverse world. This places practical, theological responsibilities on us, whether we have immediate neighbours of other faiths or not.

We believe in a God who loves the whole world and has a purpose for it which embraces all people. We are also part of a world Church. Christians in many parts of the world face issues connected with inter-faith relations on a day-to-day basis. Issues of pressing concern to Christians in one place must be of concern to other parts of the body of Christ. If we affirm this, we cannot say that the beliefs and practices of the millions who speak of God or the transcendent in a different way from us are of no interest. On the contrary, the way we articulate our beliefs and conceive of God must take them into account.

> Issues of pressing concern to Christians in one place must be of concern to other parts of the body of Christ.

Our practice should rest on this theological responsibility. Even if there are no people of other faiths near us, we can learn about what they believe. We will then become better equipped to respond with discernment when opportunities for direct inter-faith encounter arise or when we hear about other faiths through the media. We will also understand better the opportunities and challenges facing Christians who live in situations of religious diversity. Learning about other faiths may also challenge us to a deeper understanding of our own faith and why it is important to us.

Ways forward

☐ **Take responsibility to learn about at least one faith other than Christianity.**

☐ **Find out if there are centres or places of worship of people of other faiths near you. Or look at the 2001 Census statistics (http://www.statistics.gov.uk/census2001) to find out what the spread of religious affiliation is in your region.**

☐ **Organise visits to the places of worship of people of other faiths, in the nearest town that has such places of worship.**

Is there scriptural support for inter-faith dialogue?

This question arises because of the importance of the Bible for Christians. Whether something is "in the Bible" is not the only reason for Christians to take an interest in a topic. But nearly all Christians hold that the Bible can contribute something useful to our thinking on the issues and questions that arise in our lives. For many Christians, the Bible is the most important source of insight.

People may say

☐ "Yes, the Bible is itself a record of a people constantly engaged in dialogue with people of different beliefs."

☐ "Yes, the Bible gives us principles to work with. Though it's mostly a handbook for a particular people, 'the people of God', it provides principles for any situation."

☐ "No, but the Bible is not that kind of book. You can't expect it to have answers to everything. Inter-faith dialogue, as we now understand it, is a new thing, so you shouldn't expect the Bible to address it."

☐ "No, that's why this is such a difficult question!"

To consider

This question relates to the fundamental issue of how Christians use the Bible. The fact is that Christians use the Bible in many different ways. As noted in the Methodist Conference report *A Lamp to My Feet and a Light to My Path* (1998), at least seven different models of biblical authority are at work when Christians use the Bible. They are not mutually exclusive, but they are not all compatible either. In other words, use of the Bible is an area of Christian thought and spirituality where Christians really do disagree. No Christian, however, disregards the Bible altogether. To be Christian, you have to do some wrestling with it.

The question whether there is scriptural support for inter-faith dialogue will be heard differently by Christians, depending on the way that they use the Bible on any matter of faith. People who look to the Bible as the main source of Christian thought and belief will want to be reassured that the Bible provides primary guidelines with which a Christian can operate. People who stress the Bible's time-boundedness are more likely to say that, whatever the sense in which biblical writers were involved in inter-faith dialogue, it's going to be very different now.

Passages that deal with "insiders" and "outsiders" are the most relevant when looking for biblical help on the question of inter-faith relations. These passages will be read by different people within the framework of the differences in approach. Religions handle basic questions of human identity – individual and corporate. It is therefore not surprising to find both testaments of

> Passages that deal with "insiders" and "outsiders" are the most relevant.

the Christian Bible offering texts that are preoccupied by community boundaries: who's in "the people of God" and who isn't?; and how are outsiders to be treated? At one moment there is firm boundary-setting (Ezra 9 – 10; Nehemiah 13; 1 Corinthians 7, 8 and 11:14). At the next moment the activity of God beyond the identifiable people of God is being celebrated (Isaiah 45) and the borders seem more fluid (Isaiah 56:1-8; Matthew 21:28-32; Galatians 3:28-9).

The way in which the Bible portrays relationships between God's people and outsiders is, therefore, not always clear-cut. The Bible can be read as the story of how a people who believe themselves chosen by God struggle to clarify and work with their identity in the face of much opposition. It need not, however, be read as the story of a people who believe that they always know what is right. Indeed, in the light of the prophetic tradition, into which Jesus' own ministry fits, it is advisable to read the Bible as the story of a people who frequently get it wrong. The story is one of interaction between the people of God, as understood in Jewish and Christian terms, and other peoples.

Scriptural support for inter-faith dialogue may therefore be best understood less in terms of the provision of neat guidelines and more in the form of the Bible's provision of a rich fund of literary material with which contemporary Christians must wrestle. As communities of Christians interacting with all sorts of other groups (not just other religious groups), Christians must struggle with issues to do with identity and openness. For all human communities, religions included, it has always been so. And the inter-faith situation we find ourselves in now may mean that certain biblical texts come alive for us in new ways.

> Christians must struggle with issues to do with identity and openness.

Ways forward

- ☐ **Read the Bible more, and read it critically. In other words, ask questions of its stories and accept the challenge of comparing and contrasting parts of the Bible that don't seem to square up.**

- ☐ **Make sure you are clear in your own mind how you use the Bible in general. Keep in discussion with Christians who think differently – you will all benefit.**

- ☐ **Be realistic about what the Bible can and cannot do. Christians will disagree as to how concrete "biblical principles" can be, and how practically they can be applied. But don't expect the Bible to be able to answer directly the specific questions you have to face today. Its last text was completed over 1900 years ago.**

Why should we be tolerant when there are countries where Christianity is not tolerated alongside other faiths or where Christians are persecuted?

Most Christians perceive Britain as having a commitment to freedom of religion, which it can be proud of. In contrast, some countries are seen as places where persecution of Christians is rife. Missionary activity or the building of churches may be forbidden there, and violence against Christians may lie close to the surface.

It is known that, in such places, Christians, and especially converts to Christianity, maintain their witness at great personal cost. The question that follows is whether it is "right" to show tolerance to people of other faiths in Britain, when those faiths have shown intolerance to Christians elsewhere.

People may say

☐ "We are letting down our Christian sisters and brothers elsewhere if we talk to the kind of people who are persecuting them."

☐ "To meet intolerance with intolerance can never offer a Christian witness."

☐ "It is unrealistic to expect other countries to be as open as we are."

To consider

The intolerance and violence that can be fostered by religious conviction are a global concern and have been for much of human history. An easy way to respond is to meet intolerance with yet more intolerance, but this should not be the Christian way.

> Christians have been guilty of intolerance.

It should be remembered that Christians have been guilty of intolerance. For example, Jews were expelled from Britain in 1290 and were not allowed to return until almost 400 years later, after the Civil War (1642-48). In the present, there are communities and groups worldwide that still see Christianity as imperialistically intolerant, because of its link with the globalising forces of the West. And in Britain, in the last decade, there have been attacks on synagogues, mosques, gurdwaras, Hindu temples and other places of worship. Not all, but some of these have been carried out by Christians. The Runnymede Trust in 1998 published *Islamophobia: a challenge to us all*, a report that highlighted the fear and hatred of Islam in British society.

Awareness that Christians have been guilty of intolerance should be combined with confidence that Christians also have values and theological resources that can contribute to harmony and fruitful co-existence. In order to mobilise these resources, we should rigorously ask ourselves what kind of society we want Britain to be. Do we want its values to be dependent on the worst practices of intolerance in other

> Christians also have values and theological resources that can contribute to harmony.

countries? Or do we want Britain to be a place where there is space for freedom and for minorities? Do we want to erect barriers against people who believe differently from us, or do we wish to work with all who seek a harmonious Britain, rooted in common values such as respect and compassion?

This reflection should take into account the fact that respect for some practices of people of other faiths is already enshrined in Britain's legal system. For instance, the wearing of a turban has a deep religious meaning for many Sikh men. Because of this, Sikh men are exempt from the law that requires motorcyclists to wear crash helmets.

Representatives from nine faiths in Britain joined together in a Shared Act of Reflection and Commitment on 1 January 2000, at the Palace of Westminster. The "Act of Commitment" spoken on this occasion is reproduced below. It is a striking expression of the values that can unite all people of faith for the good of Britain and the world. It also leads beyond tolerance towards respect and trust between faiths.

An Act of Commitment

Faith community representatives:
  In a world scarred by the evils of war, racism,
  injustice and poverty, we offer this joint Act of
  Commitment as we look to our shared future.
All:
  We commit ourselves,
  as people of many faiths,
  to work together for the common good,
  uniting to build a better society,
  grounded in values and ideals we share:

      community,
      personal integrity,
      a sense of right and wrong,
      learning, wisdom and love of truth,
      care and compassion,
      justice and peace,
      respect for one another,
      for the earth and its creatures.

  We commit ourselves,
  in a spirit of friendship and co-operation,
  to work together
  alongside all who share our values and ideals,
  to help bring about a better world
  now and for generations to come.

Ways forward

☐ **Take whatever action you can to improve the human rights of people of every background, wherever they are abused, at home or abroad.**

☐ **Find out about countries where Christians are persecuted and pray for them.**

☐ **Work with partner churches overseas to understand and support them in the issues they face. For example, use the resources produced by the World Church Office of the Methodist Church.**

☐ **Try to break, rather than contribute to, cycles of intolerance, by working for trust and respect between faiths.**

Why does it always seem to be Christians who take the initiative in inter-faith dialogue?

A commonly held perception is that it is only Christians who are really interested in inter-faith dialogue; that it is Christians who have always taken the first step and who do most of the work to keep dialogue going. In some cases it is noted that, when Christians arrange visits to places of worship of other faiths, the people of those faiths do not ask, in return, to visit churches and learn about Christianity. This can nurture a sense of injustice, resentment or even superiority.

People may say

☐ "Perhaps we were the first in the past. But that's not true now."

☐ "It's true. Those of other religious traditions don't ever make the first move."

☐ "Christians must take the first step, as the majority faith community in Britain."

☐ "Surely the gospel is about making the first move towards 'the stranger'."

To consider

In 1942, both Jews and Christians were involved in founding one of the earliest inter-faith organisations in Britain, the Council of Christians and Jews (CCJ). In the present, organisations such as the Islamic Foundation in Leicester, the Muslim Council of Britain, the Network of Sikh Organisations, the Buddhist Society, the Baha'i Community of the UK and the National Council of Hindu Temples actively seek to promote good inter-faith relations, as members of The Inter Faith Network for the United Kingdom. It is therefore not true to say that only Christians are taking the initiative in inter-faith relations.

At a local level, however, Christians may appear to have done most of the initiating. Sociological factors are relevant here. The first priority for communities of faith, newly arrived in Britain, was identity-formation. Finding a place for worship, building internal bonds of friendship and commitment, and standing together against the discrimination that many experienced were more important than inter-faith dialogue. And at first the influence of these communities, and perhaps their confidence, were weak. It is not surprising, therefore, that Christians, the majority faith community, were the first to move, putting into action the biblical principle of hospitality, as disciples of a God who makes the first moves towards us.

Ways forward

☐ Do not be afraid of being the first to extend a hand of friendship.

☐ Find out what other communities of faith are actually doing in your area.

☐ Bear in mind that the first moves of others may be different from ours.

Do people involved in inter-faith dialogue want us to believe that all faiths are the same?

This question arises out of popular perceptions about inter-faith conversation. From the outside, it can look as though differences between faiths become non-existent when some inter-faith enthusiasts get together. The message appears to be: in spite of our different symbols, our core beliefs are the same. What then seems to arise is a new religion: interfaith.

People may say

"They do, and it's dangerous. Christianity is like no other faith. If all faiths could become one, there would be no point in being a Christian."

"No they don't. They simply know that the work of the Holy Spirit can be seen in all faiths."

"Of course they do – even if they say they don't!"

"Of course they do – and why not? If we believe in One God, there should be one religion."

To consider

If all religions were the same, there would be little point in dialogue. It would not be inter-faith dialogue at all. It would be conversation within one faith. People enter inter-faith dialogue and encounter for different reasons. Where there is conflict between religions, dialogue may be a practical necessity, to defuse tension. In this case, the starting point is difference. In other contexts, dialogue may be seen as a respectful and courteous debate about divergent truth claims. Here, again, difference is the starting point. Others prefer to seek common ethical ground, to promote co-operation between faiths on social issues. Yet others enter dialogue with the belief that ultimate truth is beyond all religions. Dialogue therefore becomes a pilgrimage towards truth, undertaken together with people of other faiths. And then there are people who simply want to discover what their neighbours of other faiths believe and practise so that they can be better neighbours. Within these groups there may be some people who believe that all faiths are the same. In practice, it is not likely to be many. For, within every faith, certain things are held to be unique. Although faiths converge in many ways, the differences between them are simply too apparent to play down.

Some inter-faith organisations and centres have taken the strategic decision to separate the "inter" and "faith" in their titles, simply in order to counter the view that inter-faith activity is about creating a new entity called "interfaith". For example: The Inter Faith Network for the United Kingdom; The London Inter Faith Centre; the Churches' Commission for Inter Faith Relations; the Methodist Inter Faith Relations Committee.

Ways forward

☐ **Expect to find both similarities and differences when you meet people of other faiths.**

☐ **Affirm similarities with joy and respect. Approach differences with respect, courtesy and a willingness to listen and learn.**

☐ **Ask yourself why it is so important for Christianity to be different.**

Are we compromising our faith through having dialogue with people of other faiths?

At all times the Church seeks to be true to its calling. Some Christians fear that the Christian faith may be watered down or distracted from its main concerns and beliefs by paying attention to dialogue with people of other faiths. The Great Commission at the end of Matthew is sometimes cited: "Go therefore and make disciples of all nations, baptising them in the name of the Father and of the Son and of the Holy Spirit" (Matthew 28:19).

People may say

☐ "Our faith will get diluted, because we'll be under pressure from non-Christian influences."

☐ "Not at all. When I'm asked questions in dialogue about my own faith, I have to think about it like I've never done before."

☐ "Why is 'compromise' a bad word? Faith changes anyway."

☐ "Christians do have to keep apart from others at times (I John 5:21). Otherwise, how can your own faith develop?"

To consider

There are passages in both testaments of the Bible that express concern about other gods and urge separation from those who worship them (Deuteronomy 29:25-6; 1 Kings 8:53, 9:8-9; 2 Corinthians 6:17). These cannot be disregarded, even if some of the texts now carry unwelcome overtones. Such passages express a deep concern that people preserve the integrity of their faith and obedience to God. They were written in circumstances when people were under pressure, and sometimes persecuted for their faith. Christians sometimes are, or feel they are, in a similar situation today, even in Britain.

Something important happens when people of like mind and belief meet together. They consolidate their belief as they celebrate it and reflect on it together. They affirm their identity. They also distinguish themselves from others who think and believe differently. However, we must resist assuming that consolidation of identity and belief should make Christians so separate from others that dialogue becomes a bad thing. On the contrary, our belief in God should send us into relationship with others, with clarity of faith, the strength to share it and the humility to listen to others. For those who are in Christ have nothing to fear.

> Our belief in God should send us into relationship with others.

So there is no question of Christians betraying their faith or the sacrifice of Christ by entering into dialogue with people of other faiths. Dialogue is part of what it means to be human. It offers Christians a unique opportunity to express what they believe, scrutinising it with theological rigour and often clarifying it further in the process. The other side, of course, is that Christians must be

vulnerable enough to listen to what is presented by people of other traditions and to scrutinise this with equal theological rigour. Some Christians testify that their participation in a dialogue of this kind, far from compromising their faith, has enhanced or renewed it. For it offers Christians the opportunity both to talk openly about Jesus Christ and their experience of him, and to hear from people of other faiths.

It is the hearing that, for some people, might imply the possibility of their Christian faith being compromised, through being influenced by others. However, to know about another faith is not the same as to believe in it or to disbelieve our own faith. And to find truth in another faith, through listening with humility, is not to deny the truth of our own.

Ways forward

☐ **Recognise the responsibility we have as members of the body of Christ to move into relationship with others.**

☐ **Do not be afraid of sharing the hope that is in you.**

☐ **Share in inter-faith dialogue in order to receive as well as to give.**

Do people of different faiths worship the same God?

If all people are worshipping the one God, then all religions could be encouraged to merge. But different religions exist. This may suggest that it is not the same God that is being worshipped. Traditions that hold to belief in one God will therefore have to conclude that others are not worshipping God at all, or will have to offer some account of why the one God is being worshipped in such different ways.

Behind this question lie one concern and one frequent assumption. The concern is: what if "we" have got God wrong? (For therefore some other tradition must have got God more "right".) The frequent assumption is: "we", obviously, have got God right, so the only question is the degree to which other religions must have got God wrong.

People may say

☐ "There's only one God and that's that!"

☐ "I really do know God. I can't say whether or not those in other religions do. But if they do, then they can surely only know the same God that I know."

☐ "Only Christians really know God. Anyone else who feels they do must be mistaken. Or, if they do get to know God, it'll be through Christ, even if they don't know that."

☐ "The religions really are different. This means that there are many 'gods'. But there's only one God. The one true God is beyond all religions."

To consider

References to the "same God" imply that there may be more than one God. Monotheists believe that there is only one God. As monotheists, Christians seek to clarify what it means to worship the one God, and are keen to find out who is truly worshipping God. It does not follow from belief in one God that there can only be one true group of worshippers, i.e. only one true religion. Nor does it follow that anyone who claims to worship the one true God is indeed a true worshipper. But the conviction that there is one true God is far-reaching as an aspect of human belief and practice. It means that the whole of creation is related to the one God.

Christianity attaches great significance to the concept of revelation, and is not alone in doing this. For Christians, there can be no talk of God without God having made God's self known to creation (e.g. Psalms 24:1-2; 104:24-30; Acts 17:26-8; Romans 1:19-20). But although Christian claims to be in touch with God are based on revelation, this does not mean that God is revealed to Christians alone. Appeals to a doctrine of revelation do not of themselves answer questions about how you know that someone truly worships God.

All believers within theistic religions use concepts, ideas and images of God to express the nature of their relationship with God. Much of the disagreement between religious traditions boils down to differences in this area. This does not mean that all people are really worshipping the one God, while simply using different images. Only God can ultimately know whether people are. No human being can stand outside of all religions in order to answer the question. However, it cannot be concluded from this that anyone's view about God is as good as anyone else's. It simply means that the task of working out who and what

God is, and what God is like, is very difficult. We should also remember that particular images of God (visual and verbal) can become especially significant within and across religions. Sometimes, attachment to particular images becomes idolatrous: concepts, ideas and images cease to be acknowledged as such and the reality of God is lost sight of.

It is essential, then, to recognise the difference between a *concept* of God and the *reality* of God. People can always learn more about God, however much they believe they "really have" encountered God. Who is God, really? How can we know it is really God we have encountered? How can we tell the true God from pale imitations (and from idols)? These questions lie at the heart of the biblical tradition (Exodus 20:4-6; Acts 19:23-41; Romans 1:21-3) and also at the heart of inter-faith encounter and dialogue. It is unlikely that the line between true and false images and understandings of God falls neatly between one religion and another. Evidence from the Bible and Christian history shows that bad beliefs and false notions of God emerge in both Judaism and Christianity, and suggests that this is probably true of all religions.

Belief in one God, alongside the existence of many long-standing religious traditions, does not mean that belief in God is simply a matter of tapping into a single tradition at any point. This would amount to indifference to the particular emphases and practices of religions. People who convert from one religion to another discover continuities and discontinuities in their experience of God. Converts to Christianity find something fresh in the recognition of God as the Father of Jesus Christ. In Christian perspective, the discovery of God's identity as trinity may be deemed the profoundest insight into God that a human being can attain. But there is a difference between demanding that all affirm God as trinity and recognising that believers in other traditions might glimpse what, in Christian terms, coheres with a belief in God as trinity. All beliefs about God are contained within particular frameworks. Though God lies beyond all religion and all religions (and may even be called "the Real" or "The Ultimate"), human beings need words and images in order to have some sense of who and what the transcendent God is.

Christians are by definition trinitarian theists and have a responsibility to articulate their experience of God in such terms. Appeals to God's self-revelation will be made. But such claims are to be made with care. All religious believers must make the best sense of their experience of God, noticing carefully where what they say agrees with and differs from experiences of God expressed in other traditions. Christians inevitably respond to practices and beliefs of other religious traditions on the grounds of Christian theology and practice. "When Christ is not named" could be offered as a criterion for assuming that something is "not Christian" and therefore "not to do with God". This does not follow, on two levels. Christ may be present even when not named. And God is clearly at work in the world not only in Christianity. Therefore, to ask what people of other traditions are seeking *in their own terms* to do and say may prove the more Christian action. Many people of other faiths claim that they do worship the one true God. Such claims are to be respected, even whilst Christian insights are to be upheld and offered as part of an inter-faith encounter.

Ways forward

☐ **Start from the assumption that those in traditions other than Christianity may have something to contribute to your understanding of the one true God.**

☐ **Don't assume that every movement that calls itself a religion inevitably commends the same concept of God as you yourself carry.**

Is there one truth? If so, why does God say different things to different people?

People of different faiths may or may not be worshipping the one God. But why are there different religions in the first place? Even saying that all the truth we need to know is to be found in the Bible is confusing, as the Bible seems to say different things on some issues. Across the many religions of the world, differences in views about people's social standing or caste, about food and about the status of women can run very deep.

People may say

- ☐ "'God' is simply another name for truth, so there has to be a single truth behind all things."

- ☐ "There is truth, and it's the Christians who know what it is."

- ☐ "There's no way that Christians alone have the truth. There are different religions simply because that's what human beings are like."

- ☐ "There is no truth, only truths. God is beyond us all. Different religions are linked to particular places and times anyway."

To consider

Belief in one God coheres readily with the notion of a single truth: the one God is the source of all truth. God and truth can then be deemed available and accessible, and knowable in the world, because of this. Christians link this claim particularly with the coming of Jesus Christ and the presence of the Holy Spirit in the world.

But truth may not always be easily accessible. Truth may always take the form of "truths" and not be experienced in pure form. Truth is always grounded in everyday life. There is a similar distinction between the reality of God and concepts and images of God. To speak of revelation reminds us that truth and God-talk are not merely human invention. Believers are grasped by God, and by truth, more than the other way round. However much we may seek, somehow we are found first. Truth finds us (we have

> Truth may always take the form of "truths" and not be experienced in pure form.

insights, inspiration, brainwaves). It finds us in the context of the everyday. When we respect the fact that truth is received in particular settings and frameworks of thought and belief, we become aware how different apprehensions of truth may be. Diversity results.

This does not mean that we end up simply with "what's true for you" and "what's true for me" and that nothing really matters. Religions exist as one of the forms of human living concerned to search for truth. They make that search count in the middle of daily living, through being a combination of belief and practice in relation to ultimate values and issues. It is for this reason that inter-faith encounter can be so passionate: truth matters, and matters for daily living. It is a different matter to

go on to say that "we" (Christians, Sikhs, Hindus or whoever) alone fully know who or what that one source of truth is. Christians know enough: as much as God has chosen to reveal. Why, though, does God say different things to different people? Why does one truth, deriving from the one God, not simply produce one religion?

The diversity of concrete and particular apprehensions of truth and the very different contexts in which God's self-revelation is experienced and articulated suggest that encounter with God may not be expressed easily and uniformly. There is a deep Christian insight that informs this particularity and diversity: incarnation. The incarnation refers to the particular revelation of God in Jesus Christ. But interpretation of the doctrine has also led many Christians to note how the incarnation informs Christian understanding of God's involvement in the world more generally: through very specific and concrete circumstances of living. Why, then, does God say different things to different people? In the end, because God reveals God's self in incarnate form, and because human beings are created to participate freely, by the Holy Spirit, in God's creation, in many and diverse settings, with all the risks and challenges involved.

Ways forward

☐ **Remember that others think they have the truth too.**

☐ **Respect the fact that different ways of accessing truth may say something profound about the richness and diversity of God.**

☐ **Be prepared to struggle with tough questions. Truth matters. To accept that "all is relative" (to time and place) doesn't make you a relativist!**

Are there any religious groups that we cannot have dialogue with?

Christians from communities that have been at the receiving end of discrimination or violence from another religious group often find it impossible to think of dialogue with that group. This may be the feeling, for example, of some British Christians from minority ethnic communities, who are in touch with painful situations of discrimination in other parts of the world. For other Christians, this question may arise in the context of the bad press that some New Religious Movements (NRMs) receive. The question raises the difficult issue of whether there are limits to dialogue.

People may say

☐ "Surely there is a difference between the great world religions and other groups?"

☐ "I'm all in favour of dialogue, but what about some of the new groups that brainwash people? Am I expected to speak to them?"

☐ "It all depends on whether the people we are talking to are willing to listen and discuss things rationally."

To consider

At the heart of this question is the issue of criteria for dialogue. In Britain today, formal inter-faith dialogue at a national level is usually confined to representatives of the nine faiths that belong to the Inter Faith Network for the United Kingdom: Baha'is, Buddhists, Christians, Jains, Jews, Hindus, Muslims, Sikhs and Zoroastrians. There is a Code of Conduct that informs and sets the parameters for dialogue at this level (see right and Appendix 1).

Many local inter-faith groups and Councils of Faiths have a similar code of conduct. Those who refuse to adhere to it can be asked to leave the group. At this level, especially in informal inter-faith groups (as opposed to groups with strict rules concerning representation), a wider spectrum of religious affiliation can be expected, including members of NRMs and the Pagan Federation.

The codes stress respect and courtesy. Dialogue is possible when all partners are able to listen to and respect what the other is saying, and to share what they want to say without aggression or coercion. If these principles are present, we should be willing to have dialogue. This should be so even when we may fear that we will not agree with much that our partners in dialogue are saying.

> Dialogue is possible when all partners are able to listen to and respect what the other is saying, and to share what they want to say without aggression or coercion.

If these principles are not present, true dialogue is impossible. Other forms of encounter and conversation may be possible, but cannot really be called dialogue. In situations where inter-faith encounter may generate hurt, violence or resentment, the skills of conflict resolution may be necessary, perhaps involving the work of a mediator.

Ways forward

☐ **Beware of denying any person the right to speak to you, solely on the grounds of the beliefs they hold.**

☐ **Base any decision not to engage in dialogue with a particular group on concrete evidence, not on hearsay or preconceptions based on prejudice.**

☐ **Honour the same ground rules whatever dialogue you are engaged in, for example the willingness to listen.**

Code of Conduct for Dialogue

The following is an extract from the Inter Faith Network Code of Conduct, adopted by the Methodist Conference in 1994. (See Appendix 1 for the complete Code of Conduct.)

When we talk about matters of faith with one another, we need to do so with sensitivity, honesty and straightforwardness. This means:

- **recognising that listening as well as speaking is necessary for a genuine conversation;**
- **being honest about our beliefs and religious allegiances;**
- **not misrepresenting or disparaging other people's beliefs and practices;**
- **correcting misunderstanding or misrepresentations not only of our own but also of other faiths whenever we come across them;**
- **being straightforward about our intentions;**
- **accepting that in formal inter faith meetings there is a particular responsibility to ensure that the religious commitment of all those who are present will be respected.**

All of us want others to understand and respect our views. Some people will also want to persuade others to join their faith. In a multi faith society where this is permitted, the attempt should always be characterised by self-restraint and a concern for the other's freedom and dignity. This means:

- **respecting another person's expressed wish to be left alone;**
- **avoiding imposing ourselves and our views on individuals or communities who are in vulnerable situations in ways which exploit these;**
- **being sensitive and courteous;**
- **avoiding violent action or language, threats, manipulation, improper inducements, or the misuse of any kind of power;**
- **respecting the right of others to disagree with us.**

Should our attitude to Judaism be different from our attitude to other faiths?

There is a special relationship between Christians and Jews. Jesus was a Jew, and, historically, Christianity was born out of Judaism; both faiths see themselves as part of the story of God's covenant with Israel. Christians share with Jews what Christians call the Old Testament and Jews call *Tanakh*, although they interpret it differently; Christians have to decide how they understand God's promises to Israel and covenant with her, as witnessed in those scriptures.

For these reasons, there always has been dialogue and debate between Jews and Christians, and many would feel that this relationship must continue to be the most important one to explore. However, Christians from backgrounds in other religions, for example from traditional religions in Africa, sometimes feel that, in their context, it is not Judaism but the religious tradition of their own past that should be the most meaningful partner in dialogue.

People may say

"Christians will always be bound together with Jews as their brothers and sisters."

"In Romans 11:25-8 Paul declares that God's promises to Israel can never be broken."

"Historically, Christianity is the fulfilment of Judaism, but Christianity also completes the revelation of God present in other faiths."

"The Abrahamic faiths – and that includes Islam – share belief in the same God, and the same fundamental family values: we should seek to work together."

"The persecution and murder of Jews in the Christian West mean that Christians have a particular obligation to dialogue and reconciliation with Jews."

To consider

Jesus and the earliest disciples were Jews, and Christianity emerged out of Judaism over a period of time, more slowly in some areas than in others. Like any breakaway movement, early Christianity was sometimes very harsh towards its mother faith, and often misrepresented it: indeed, there are still many false conceptions of Judaism, as a religion shaped by the demands of obedience to the law. Centuries of Christian preaching, often using the Jews as a model of faithlessness, created a context where Jews could be persecuted and even murdered in Christian towns and cities; this is one of the roots that made the *Shoah* or Holocaust possible in "Christian Europe".

Since then, scholars have become much more aware of the history of Christian anti-Judaism or anti-semitism and have sought ways towards reconciliation. They have also learned more about the many contexts where Jews and Christians lived closely together and learned from each other. In fact, throughout the history of Christianity there has been dialogue between Jews and Christians, sometimes more friendly, sometimes more hostile.

For Jesus, God was the God of Israel's history and experience, whom he, like other Jews, called "father". Christians claimed that Jesus fulfilled the prophets' hopes of God's visitation of the people and the world. Paul taught that Gentile converts were grafted into the olive tree of God's election of Israel, so that they too were heirs to the covenant promises. Later Christians debated whether the (new) covenant into which they were brought meant that God's covenant with Israel had come to an end, or whether it was part of and continuous with that covenant. As Christians have reflected more on the nature of God's faithfulness, and on the testimony of Jewish faith even in the face of hostility and persecution, recent ecumenical statements have recognised the importance of emphasising God's faithfulness to God's covenant with Israel; although modern theologians still debate whether we should speak of one covenant or of two.

Particular individuals and churches may find that, in their setting, their closest partner in dialogue is the faith of their neighbours or the faith from which they have come. However this cannot replace the fact that, for the whole Church, through history and in the world, God worked and made God's self known through Israel, and through Jesus, born as a Jew. This suggests that there is not just one model for understanding all other religions from a Christian perspective. However, perhaps the way that Christians have learnt to work alongside Jews, but also to wrestle with the theological questions, means that Jewish-Christian dialogue can become a touchstone and a school for dialogue with other traditions.

> Perhaps ...
> Jewish-Christian
> dialogue can become a
> touchstone and a
> school for dialogue
> with other traditions.

Ways forward

☐ **Find out more about the work of the Council of Christians and Jews (CCJ): there may be a local branch near you. The CCJ also sponsors dialogue with Islam, especially on shared concerns of social and communal life.**

☐ **Do not misrepresent Judaism, either in the past or as a living tradition today.**

☐ **Ask a Jewish lay person or teacher/religious leader to tell your study group what Abraham means to them.**

☐ **Find out more about the Holocaust (*Shoah*) and about the faith and experience of survivors of the concentration camps, or their children. Many churches observe or share in the activities that take place around the Jewish Holocaust Memorial Day in April or the national Holocaust Memorial Day on 27 January.**

☐ **Share a Bible study on Romans 9 – 11.**

We hear so much about Muslims and the growth of Islam. What are we to make of it all?

Islam is, after Christianity, the world's second largest religion. For all sorts of reasons there are growing numbers of Muslims in Europe, North America and Australia, as well as in the established Muslim world covering much of Africa and Asia. Since 11 September 2001 (when passenger jets hijacked by Islamic terrorists were aimed at targets in the United States) Muslims and the Islamic faith have rarely been out of the news. Some politicians have presented Islam as a threat to Western values and security. Some religious leaders have stereotyped Islam as a violent religion. There has been an understandable increase in "Islamophobia" – an irrational fear of Islam. Not surprisingly, people have asked a myriad of questions about Islam and about Muslims.

People may say

☐ "The terrorists responsible for 9/11 and other atrocities were Muslim fanatics: Islam threatens our Christian civilisation and way of life."

☐ "Muslims in our community are decent, devout, God-fearing people. They care more than we do about family values. You have to respect that."

☐ "I hear that many Muslim countries are intolerant of Christians. Churches are burned down and Christians are fearful for their homes and jobs and even their lives."

☐ "Islam and Christianity are both religions of peace. Why can't we work together to make the world safer and stop the escalating violence?"

To consider

Islam traces its faith back to Abraham (it is often referred to as one of the "Abrahamic" faiths) and, like Judaism and Christianity, it is strongly monotheistic. The profession of faith, "I testify that there is no God but Allah and Muhammad is Allah's messenger", is the first of five basic practices known as the "Five Pillars" of Islam. Although the Qur'an, the holy book of Islam, understands God in significantly different ways from Christians and Jews, nevertheless it clearly states that God has guided humanity through the revelation contained in the Jewish and Christian scriptures.

Islam is, with Christianity and Judaism, a "religion of the book". The Qur'an contains stories from the Old Testament and has much to say about Jesus, who is respected as a prophet and messenger of God. But Muslims find the Christian belief in God as Trinity blasphemous. God is one and uncreated and so cannot be associated with the created order and with human history. For Muslims, the Qu'ran itself is God's revelation. Written, read, sung and chanted in Arabic, it is central to the life and prayer of Muslims from birth to death.

The words "fundamentalist" and "fundamentalism" have often been used to describe Muslims and their attitude. For Muslims, the text of the Qur'an is given – it cannot be challenged. Its authority is complete and, in that narrow sense, a devout Muslim is a fundamentalist. But in the Muslim world there are many approaches to the interpretation of the Qur'an and differing views about how it applies to life and situations today. In another sense, "fundamentalism" is about maintaining or recovering the fundamentals of a faith. In the last 200 years there have been a number of "renewal" movements in Islam.

The history of Muslim-Christian relations is long and complex. Both Islam and Christianity are missionary by nature and aim to convert non-believers. While there have been occasions when each has attempted to use war to expand, there have also been centuries of peaceful co-existence. Like Christianity, Islam is not monolithic. The differences of approach between Sunna and Shi'a go back to very soon after the death of the Prophet Muhammad. A minority of Muslims today are Arabs, and the five countries with the largest Muslim populations (over half of all the Muslims in the world) are Indonesia, India, Pakistan, Bangladesh and China.

Where relations are difficult and there is violence, it is usually very hard to separate political, economic and cultural issues from religious ones and it is all too easy to use the words "Muslim" and "Islamic" for what are actually much more complex realities. A number of factors can have a bearing, including past events, the proportions of Muslims and Christians in the community or nation, and where power lies or is believed to lie. Greed or grievance is much more likely than religion to be the cause of conflict, but religion may increase the risk or intensify it.

> Greed or grievance is much more likely than religion to be the cause of conflict.

Each situation is specific but, because of migration and increasingly rapid global communications, what happens in one part of the world can affect relationships elsewhere. A misunderstanding of *jihad* (strife or struggle) has led some people to see a unified global struggle of Muslims rather than a number of more local situations. The primary sense of *jihad* is the personal struggle to live as a good Muslim. A secondary sense relates to striving to spread or defend the faith; but most Muslims today would believe that a *jihad* of the sword was wrong. Osama bin Laden (and Al-Qaeda), in 1996 and 1998, reacted to the alleged United States invasion of the holy places of Jerusalem, Mecca and Medina with a statement that it was every Muslim's duty to respond to this declaration of war on Allah, Muhammad and Muslims. Most Muslims reject this interpretation of *jihad*.

Realism will dismiss any too easy suggestion that there are no present difficulties for Christians in relation to Islam, but Christians will want to seek the truth, recognising its complexity. The long history of dialogue with Islam; the shared (if not identical) concerns about the sanctity of human life, the importance of the family and spiritual values in the life of society; and commitment to seeking justice and peace are all incentives to continuing to seek to understand and relate to each other as people of faith in a violent world.

Ways forward

☐ **Read an English translation of the Qur'an or of selections from it.**

☐ **When you read newspaper reports that link Muslims generally, or Islam as a whole, with violence, terrorism or fundamentalism, ask whether these are likely to be accurate or truthful.**

☐ **Meet Muslim neighbours or local Muslim groups (perhaps through a local inter-faith group).**

☐ **Look for opportunities to work with Muslims and others on shared community concerns (for example, with a local group supporting asylum seekers).**

Do we have to think everything is good in another religion?

Some people believe that those involved in inter-faith dialogue avoid questions connected with the differences between faiths and shy away from any negative judgements, in order to avoid conflict. They themselves are worried by particular aspects of other religions, such as their apparent involvement in violence or terrorism or their treatment of women, which they perceive as oppressive. They are concerned that inter-faith dialogue may condone practices that they are unhappy about.

People may say

"How can I think everything is good in other religions? A look at the world's wars shows religion at the centre of what is wrong in the world."

"People of other faiths can be holier than us. Every faith has been touched by God."

"Inter-faith dialogue is about real issues. I would have nothing to do with it if it was only about mutual back-patting."

To consider

One of the best ways to approach this question is to look at Christianity. In spite of the love that lies at the heart of Christian self-understanding, few Christians could say that the history of Christian belief and practice has consistently demonstrated that love. Whether we look at the Crusades, the slave trade, Christian support of apartheid in South Africa, the sexual abuse of children or discrimination against women, Christianity has not been and is not blameless. And the selective use of scripture has sometimes contributed to these wrongs. Violence has been done in the name of God. Similar patterns exist in other faiths. Few religions can boast that they have lived up to their ideals.

> Few religions can boast that they have lived up to their ideals.

When we meet people of other religions, we will find things that resonate with and enrich our own convictions, and other things that do not. The latter may include both practical expressions of the faith and doctrinal beliefs. Similarly, people of other faiths, when they look at us, may not be able to sympathise or agree with everything they see.

It should also be remembered that no faith is monolithic. Within each faith, there is dialogue between people of different views. An additional consideration is that the interrelated nature of culture and religion can mean that practices that have more to do with culture may appear to be sanctioned by religion. For instance, the practice of forced marriage is found within some religious communities, but it is not legitimised by the religions

> Practices that have more to do with culture may appear to be sanctioned by religion.

themselves. Young people in Britain affected by this are now appealing to their religious traditions against oppressive cultural practices.

What should be avoided, therefore, is condemning the whole of a faith because we disagree with part of its belief or practice. Few Christians would want Christianity to be condemned through partial judgements, especially if these are rooted in incomplete evidence. It should also be borne in mind that, because a belief or practice in another faith differs from Christianity, it does not mean that it is inferior or bad. Engaging positively with what is most different between faiths can, in fact, bring unexpected insights into truth.

Ways forward

☐ **Do not judge the whole of a faith by the actions of extremists within it or by what is reported in the press.**

☐ **Do not judge the whole of a faith by what you consider are its weaknesses, or compare the best ideal in one religion with the worst practice in another.**

☐ **Do not be afraid in inter-faith dialogue to raise what you do not agree with, but remember that this is best done when trust is present.**

☐ **Be ready to be self-critical. This can help the building of trust and the level of depth gained in discussion.**

☐ **Make sure you compare like with like when discussing the differences between religions.**

Should we be willing to be changed in inter-faith dialogue?

Some Christians fear that inter-faith dialogue will be too challenging. They fear that it will strike at the root of all that they hold dear and cause them to water down what they believe. Some of these people might fear all change. Others seek ways of discerning what can be changed as a result of inter-faith dialogue and what cannot.

People may say

☐ "God has given us a simple, eternal and unchangeable faith, and I'll stand firm in it whatever happens."

☐ "Life is all about change. God does not want us to stay still. I want to be changed by meeting other faiths. And I want people of other faiths to be changed by meeting me."

☐ "My faith has grown stronger through contact with people of other faiths. If that's change, then I want more of it!"

☐ "I expect to change through my conversations with people of other faiths. But my faith will always be Christian and I will always want to share it. It's part of me."

☐ "Other faiths? They make me feel nervous. I'm afraid that what I believe in will be attacked."

To consider

In any encounter, if we do not expect to be changed, then either our participation is superficial or we are only encountering people in order to change them to our way of thinking. The former is hardly worth the name of inter-faith dialogue and the latter is a theologically deficient way of understanding human relationships. Jesus himself is shown changing through his encounters with others (for example in his conversation with the Canaanite woman in Matthew

> Openness to be changed through encounter lies at the heart of what it is to be human.

15:21-8). Openness to be changed through encounter lies at the heart of what it is to be human. And it should not be forgotten that we believe in a God who was willing to empty God's self in order to participate in the world. Listening to people of other faiths and sharing what we believe to be good news with others is likely to change us.

Saying that we should be willing to be changed through meeting people of other faiths is not the same as saying that we should be willing to change everything. In rare cases, dialogue might lead to conversion from one faith to another. In most cases, it enriches rather than radically alters our own faith. In learning more about how to share what we believe, we can be strengthened in our faith in Christ. In listening to the witness of others, we can learn and be enriched. What we learn, though, may challenge some of our theological presuppositions. If this happens, we should not avoid working through the implications, either for the Church or for our own spirituality. Throughout the history of Christianity, theology has developed and spirituality has been nurtured through humans reflecting theologically on their experience, individually or in groups.

Ways forward

☐ **Learn more about how Christianity has changed over the centuries.**

☐ **Don't fear change. Find a way to embrace it. Through coming to know what our neighbours of other faiths believe, we learn more about ourselves and can grow in our relationship to God.**

☐ **Think back within your own faith journey and consider what factors caused you to change your mind or modify your belief. Use this as a framework for understanding what encounter with other faiths might bring about.**

☐ **Remember that people of other faiths whom you encounter may be afraid of changing, or want to change, too.**

Are we betraying the sacrifice and commitment of Christians who have converted from other faiths if we do not seek the conversion of all people to Christianity?

In Britain and throughout the world there are people who have converted from other faith traditions to Christianity, and rejoice that now they know Jesus Christ as Lord. Some of these people may have suffered greatly as Christians, possibly being disowned by their family and friends or persecuted by their local community or government. Some do not find in the Church the welcome that they hoped for or the support that they need. For Christians who have heard a lot about this kind of suffering, conversations with people of other faiths that do not have an evangelistic aim may seem to belittle both the sacrifice of Jesus Christ and the courage of those who have converted to Christianity.

People may say

- "If we don't seek to convert people of other faiths, or at least hope and pray that they will come to know Jesus, we imply that conversion doesn't matter, and we cheapen the sacrifice of those who have converted."

- "If all Christians are interested in is dialogue, what about my suffering as a convert?"

- "Surely we can celebrate with converts to Christianity without expecting everyone we talk to from another faith to convert?"

- "Perhaps we don't always realise how threatened other faith communities feel by aggressive Christian missionary activity."

To consider

People convert from other faiths to Christianity and also from Christianity to other faiths. This may happen for a variety of reasons and in a variety of ways. It may be in response to missionary activity, or through meeting people of the other faith and finding friendship or support. It may be through reading or through an inspirational teacher. Conversion is always an important part of an individual's life story and it can be a sign of spiritual seeking and liveliness.

> Conversion is always an important part of an individual's life story and it can be a sign of spiritual seeking and liveliness.

Some converts bring into their new faith negative experiences and feelings about the faith they have left, and they express their criticisms forcibly. Others are more positive, seeking continuity between their different experiences of faith. It should be remembered that converts both to and from Christianity have experienced harsh treatment from people within the faith they have left.

Christians should offer welcome, support and love to those who convert to Christianity. If the converts have suffered as a result of their conversion, their courage should be recognised. However, it does not follow from this that the *aim* of inter-faith encounter should be to multiply the number of

converts. People of other faiths quickly recognise if someone they are speaking with wishes to convert them to another religion. Mistrust and anger can result.

It should be remembered that there have been times when the Church has used force or inappropriate forms of persuasion to bring in converts from other faiths, or when it has brought great pressure to bear on those who converted out. The forced conversion of Jews in European history is one example. And in the present, aggressive forms of evangelism are still being used by some Christian groups. All of this, whether it is stored in a faith's collective memory or experienced in the present, can be a source of fear, hurt and anger. The sacrifice of Jesus is not served well by Christians increasing this sense of hurt by insensitive evangelism.

Ways forward

- ☐ **Rejoice with those who have converted to Christianity, valuing what they bring to the life of the Church.**

- ☐ **Respect the decision of people who choose to leave Christianity for another faith.**

- ☐ **Learn about and pray for churches in other lands that are growing in spite of pressure or persecution.**

Are we, as Methodists, betraying our calling if we do not seek the conversion of all people to the Christian faith?

Methodism was born through the evangelistic zeal of John Wesley; his passion to make the love of God known to people who were not being touched by church structures. He called people away from "the god of this world" to the God of Jesus Christ. His message was unmistakably about conversion. Some Methodists, aware of this heritage and the fact that evangelism is one of four key tasks in the present "Calling" of the Methodist Church (alongside Worship, Learning and Caring, and Service) see respectful dialogue with people of other faiths as compromise. For surely, they feel, Methodists should be aiming above all to make more followers of Jesus Christ.

People may say

☐ "What are we called to if it is not to make more followers of Jesus Christ?"

☐ "Part of what we are called to is to see what is of God in other faiths."

☐ "More important for me than wanting people of other faiths to become Christian is to work with them to challenge injustice."

☐ "'Is thy heart right, as my heart is with thy heart? If it be, give me thine hand' – those words of John Wesley have been an inspiration to me in inter-faith relations."

To consider

Different Christian traditions have different resources to draw on when thinking about inter-faith relations. Methodists will want to look back to the work of John and Charles Wesley, and the tradition that was born through their work and thought.

John Wesley's only experience of inter-faith encounter was with Jews in Europe and with American Indians in Georgia. He also read widely. From the evidence of his journals, this included two biographies of the Prophet Muhammad. In his writings, there are paradoxes in his attitude to people of other faiths and their cultures. In "A Caution Against Bigotry" (Sermon 38), for instance, he clearly categorises the American Indians as barbarian; and in "The Imperfection of Human Knowledge" (Sermon 69), he refers to "Indostan" (India) as a dark and cruel habitation. However, in Sermon 130, "On Living Without God", whilst condemning Christians who believe in works and not faith, he writes this:

Let it be observed, I purposely add, 'to those that are under the Christian dispensation', because I have no authority from the word of God 'to judge those that are without'. Nor do I conceive any man living has a right to sentence all the heathen and Mahometan world to damnation. It is far better to leave them to him that made them, and who is 'the Father of the spirits of all flesh'; who is the God of the heathens as well as the Christians, and who hateth nothing that he hath made.

In a similar vein, at the end of Sermon 106, "On Faith", he wrote of "Heathens, Mahometans and Jews": "We may wish their lives did not shame many of us that are called Christians." And, in his

journal of Monday, 4 April 1737, there is this: "I began learning Spanish, in order to converse with my Jewish parishioners some of whom seem to be nearer the mind that was in Christ than many of those who call him Lord."

Quotations such as these last three have inspired Methodists, especially in the last 50 years, to enter inter-faith dialogue with the aim of building relationships of trust and understanding. For it is interesting to note that Wesley seeks to "converse with" his Jewish parishioners, not to "convert" them. Some Methodists would consider that the less formal "conversing" or "conversation" are better words than "dialogue" for describing what should happen when people of different faiths meet.

Methodists involved in inter-faith relations have also been inspired by the emphasis John Wesley put on prevenient grace; in other words, the grace that is active in people even before they recognise their need of it. This kind of grace, according to John Wesley, is already at work in everyone, through the Holy Spirit.

The writings of John Wesley and the hymns of Charles, though, are just one of the resources that Methodists can draw on. The Methodist tradition is continuously developing and changing and it has produced contemporary pioneers in inter-faith relations such as Wesley Ariarajah, Kenneth Cracknell, Martin Forward, Geoffrey Parrinder, Lynne Price and Pauline Webb. Our calling can therefore draw from several strands within the Methodist tradition. The evangelism that involves a direct call to others to become followers of Jesus Christ is part of that tradition. So also is "conversing with" people of other faiths, in recognition that the Holy Spirit may have gone before us.

Ways forward

- ☐ **Seize opportunities for discovery and growth in your individual faith journey.**

- ☐ **Explore what "conversing with" people of other faiths may bring.**

- ☐ **Find out more about the concept of prevenient grace.**

- ☐ **Read a few of John Wesley's sermons, for instance "A Caution Against Bigotry" (Sermon 38) and "Catholic Spirit" (Sermon 39). These can be found in *The Works of John Wesley*, Bi-Centennial Edition, John Baker (ed.), Nashville, Abingdon Press.**

- ☐ **Give thanks to God when evangelism results in people becoming followers of Jesus Christ, but do not believe that we convert others. It is the work of the Holy Spirit.**

Our Calling was adopted by the Methodist Conference of 2000:

The Church exists to increase awareness of God's presence and to celebrate God's love.

The Church exists to help people to grow and learn as Christians through mutual support and care.

The Church exists to be a good neighbour to people in need and to challenge injustice.

The Church exists to make more followers of Jesus Christ.

How should we respond to texts like John 14:6?

Verses such as John 14:6 ("Jesus said to him, 'I am the way, and the truth, and the life. No one comes to the Father except through me'.") are interpreted by some Christians to mean that people can be saved only through a conscious acknowledgement of the work of God through Jesus Christ. Other Christians challenge this understanding. Whatever interpretation is held, it is a controversial verse that is often found at the centre of Christian debate about other religions. People of other faiths may be sympathetic to the debate, alienated by it or simply puzzled.

People may say

☐ "John 14:6 states that salvation is through Christ alone. Our main task is therefore to make disciples of Christ from among all people, but we should of course be prepared to listen to others."

☐ "John 14:6 reflects a certain time and place. It cannot be applied to our situation now."

☐ "John 14:6 means that anyone who is saved is, in fact, saved through Christ, whether they know it or not."

☐ "John 14:6 is not that unusual. Many faiths have similar verses."

To consider

The responses made by Christians to verses such as John 14:6 may be exclusivist, inclusivist or pluralist. Each of these three kinds of response can take a spectrum of forms. Risking simplification: the exclusivist affirms that it is only through faith in the work of God through Jesus Christ that humans can gain salvation and be brought into a right relationship with God. The inclusivist also affirms that salvation is through Jesus Christ alone, but adds that other faiths can be vehicles for the saving grace that is in Christ. In other words, people of other faiths can be saved through Christ, without consciously knowing it. The pluralist position affirms that all religions have the potential to offer salvation; all potentially offer humans transcendent vision and human transformation. John 14:6 is appreciated for its place in the history of the Early Church, rather than for what it may say about other faiths.

Each of these positions should be respected. For this is the kind of verse that Christians need to wrestle with, precisely because there are different ways of interpreting it. Coming too quickly to a resolution of the diverse issues it raises could be counter-productive.

When reflecting on the meaning of individual texts, Christians need to recognise the importance of respecting the whole Bible as bearing witness to God's revelation. It is

> This is the kind of verse that Christians need to wrestle with, precisely because there are different ways of interpreting it.

possible to over-emphasise the importance of particular texts because they express our own particular faith convictions. John 14:6 can be paralleled with other texts that seemingly take an exclusivist position, such as John 3:16, 18 and Acts 4:11-12. The prologue to John's gospel, however, equates Jesus with the Logos, the Word, which has been active in God's creation from the beginning, as light in darkness. This suggests a more inclusivist position.

It is also important to remember that Christians read the Bible in a particular set of contexts: as twenty-first-century British Methodists; as men and women; as Asian, black and white people; as young, middle-aged and older people. These contexts condition how texts are understood. Similarly, the context of the writer of John's gospel impacted on his writing: first-century life, as a man, around the Mediterranean Sea; member of a group of believers seeking to establish itself against some opposition from already established communities. What we bring to the text now may be very different from what the Early Church brought to it.

Ways forward

- ☐ **Engage in respectful conversation with other Christians who might think differently from you about the meaning of John 14:6.**

- ☐ **See if you can find more than one commentary on John 14:6.**

- ☐ **Avoid answers that seem too easy or clear-cut.**

- ☐ **Reflect on how your own Christianity is shaped by the culture in which you live.**

Should I be trying to convert people of other faiths to Christianity?

All Christians are called to share the good news of Jesus Christ. This is what Christians place at the heart of mission. But Christians have different understandings of what this means in a multi-faith society. For some people, this is a cause of genuine confusion.

People may say

☐ "Why should we seek to convert people of other faiths to Christianity? Their own faiths can lead them to God and salvation, and many live far better lives than Christians."

☐ "I rejoice when people of other faiths convert to Christianity. But that doesn't mean I want everyone who belongs to another faith to convert."

☐ "We should seek to convert everyone to a Christian faith because this is God's will."

To consider

Christians may not agree on every point of doctrine, but they do believe that they have good news to share. The gospels present different forms of mission and witness. The Great Commission at the end of Matthew's gospel stresses the making of disciples through baptism and teaching the commandments of Jesus (Matthew 28:19-20). Paul's plea to the Romans concerning the need for people to hear and believe that Jesus Christ is Lord emphasises proclamation of the death and resurrection of Christ (Romans 10:14-15). The story of Jesus washing the feet of his

> The gospels present different forms of mission and witness.

disciples stresses loving, self-sacrificial service among the followers of Christ (John 13:1-17). The picture of Jesus as a young man sitting in the temple in Jerusalem asking questions of the wisest teachers of his day offers yet another model, rooted in inquiry and attentive listening (Luke 2:41-50). The story of Paul in Athens is a model of vigorous debate and public speaking, which builds on where people are and what they have already experienced (Acts 17:16-31).

All the passages mentioned show examples of what mission is. And all the different forms of mission, if carried out with sensitivity, can communicate today what the Christian good news is about. But the specific ways in which mission is carried out need to be appropriate to today's society.

In re-examining the Great Commission, for instance, we may have to take into account that there are also people in other faith traditions who claim that they honour or revere Jesus. Muslims, for instance, revere the prophet Isa (Arabic for Jesus) as the Promised Messiah, God's Word and a healer. Some Hindus may claim that they love and seek to follow Jesus, as well as other holy teachers. They may have a picture of Jesus in their shrine at home. Are they, therefore, already disciples? Some Methodists will wish to say yes; others, no.

Before attempting proclamation, Christians should put themselves in the shoes of a person of another faith. People of other faiths may say: "Well, I wouldn't want to have dialogue with someone who only wanted to convert me!" And surely Christians would say exactly the same if someone of another faith tried to convert them.

Within Methodism, there will continue to be different positions on the question of conversion and evangelism. Whichever position is taken, it is God who converts, through the work of the Holy Spirit. No coercion should ever be practised. Our task is to witness to the love of God and to create relationships of mutual trust and friendship with our neighbours of other faiths. And witness can take many forms. As the Eighth Principle for Dialogue and Evangelism adopted by the Methodist Conference in 1994 stated: "Methodists need to affirm a variety of vocations within the body of Christ, which affect relationships with people of other faiths."

> It is God who converts, through the work of the Holy Spirit.

Ways forward

- ☐ **Be prepared to share in truth and love, with all people, God's invitation to come to God through Jesus Christ.**

- ☐ **Remember that it is as wrong to exert pressure on a person to convert to the Christian faith as it would be to exclude a person from opportunities to respond to God through Christ.**

- ☐ **Remember that the story of Jesus is the Church's greatest gift to explore and to share; it is usually Jesus, not the churches, who fascinates others.**

- ☐ **Listen to people of other faiths as they share what is precious in their faith.**

Can people of other faiths be saved?

Salvation is one of the ways through which Christians understand their relationship to God and their hope for this life and the next. Crucially important for many Christians is whether people of other faiths can be saved and so have the same hope as themselves. For many people this is the most important question for thinking about Christian evangelism and mission.

People may say

☐ "How can there be salvation in other faiths? It is only through faith in Christ's death and resurrection that people can be saved."

☐ "God's saving action cannot be limited. Of course God can save people within other faiths."

☐ "All who seek God's ways can be saved, even if they don't acknowledge faith in Christ consciously."

☐ "The idea of salvation doesn't mean much to some faiths. We should try to learn what these faiths place at the centre."

To consider

Christians rejoice that their relationship with God rests not in their own goodness but in God's goodness to them. John Wesley expressed this as "salvation by grace through faith", drawing on texts such as Ephesians 2:8. Salvation is not simply a future hope, but is for all time. It has past, present and future dimensions. It is something God has brought about. It is being enjoyed, and it is yet to be brought to completion.

Most Christians will refer to Christ when they think of salvation. The Bible, however, provides many images of what salvation is, not all of them Christ-centred. Salvation is an important term in the Old Testament. The Psalms frequently refer to God as Saviour or Deliverer (e.g. Psalm 3:8; 35:9; 68:19; 74:2; 89:26; 118:14). So does Isaiah (e.g. 12:2-3; 25:9; 33:6; 51:6-8). In these contexts, salvation is linked with

> The Bible provides many images of what salvation is, not all of them Christ-centred.

everlasting safety and security in the midst of change and decay. It is abundance of life, joy, peace and knowledge of God. It is described in terms of the individual and of the nation.

Salvation, however, is not the only concept used in the Bible to speak of how people can come close to God. God's people are also said to be followers of the way of righteousness and to be in Christ. We can then ask what it is to be a follower of that way and what it means to be in Christ. The Beatitudes give us one model (Matthew 5:1-11; Luke 6:20-22); the parable of the sheep and the goats, another (Matthew 25:31-46). There are also other models and pictures that Christians must struggle with.

Into this can come biblical examples of God working through those who are outside the identified people of God. Cyrus of Persia, for example, is understood to be not only God's agent but God's anointed one (Isaiah 45). In the gospels, the faith of the Syro-Phoenician woman (Mark 7:24-30) and the Roman centurion (Matthew 8:5-13) is affirmed. In Acts, the spirituality of the Athenians (Acts 17:16-32) is presented as a potential stepping-stone to knowledge of the one God. These examples suggest that God works through and beyond the Church and that Christians should be cautious of judging others as amongst the righteous or unrighteous. It would be as wrong to assume that all those within other faith traditions are not saved, as it would be to claim that all Christians are living truly Christ-like lives.

It should also be remembered that salvation is a particularly Christian term. Not all faiths place salvation at the centre. For some people of other faiths, the question of whether they are saved has little meaning or relevance. Because salvation is so important to Christianity, Christians will want to explore whether people of other faiths are saved as Christians understand that. But Christians can also discover how people of other faiths understand their relationship with the divine, and the goal it leads them to.

> Salvation is a particularly Christian term. Not all faiths place salvation at the centre.

Ways forward

☐ **Explore and deepen your understanding of God's grace and salvation.**

☐ **Listen to how people of other faiths understand the meaning of life and be prepared to explain your understanding.**

How do we witness to what we believe in a multi-faith society?

For some Christians, this is perhaps the most important question of all. Much nineteenth- and early twentieth-century hymnody gave the Church a missionary model based on the assumption that the beliefs of people of other faiths were false and that Christian witness was about convincing them of this. The theology of mission has moved on. But many Christians are unsure what form of witness is now appropriate. How should Christians speak of the hope that is in them? How should they speak of the love of God?

People may say

☐ "The way we witness should always be the same, because the Good News is always the same and we must share it."

☐ "If people already have a faith, surely our witness should be different than if they haven't."

☐ "Simply showing Christian love to all is enough for me."

To consider

Christians witness when they speak about Jesus Christ and live according to his teaching. In this way, they make Christ known through word and action, and share their joy in all that has been achieved through him. Such witness has always been part of the Christian faith and will continue to be. The important question is not whether Christians should witness in a multi-faith society, but how.

In their witness, some Christians focus on showing the love of God in action, through caring service and struggling against injustice. For God is the one who sides with the victims, seeks just relationships between people, and lays emphasis on protection of the weak and hospitality to the stranger. Our action in society must reflect this. Whether the victims or the weak are Christians, of another faith or of no faith, our obligation is to side with them and protect them.

Others seek to make Christ known through conversation about faith, and the building of friendships that enable this. This is a most important part of Christian witness. Appendix 1 gives a Code of Conduct for inter-faith relations, which the Methodist Conference adopted in 1994. It stresses principles such as courtesy and respect for the beliefs of others. Such principles must form the bedrock of such witness. For, if we condemn the faith commitments of others, stereotype them or misrepresent them, it is unlikely that our listeners will detect that we are actually speaking about a God of love. This kind of witness is "false" in the sense of the ninth Commandment, "You shall not

> If we condemn the faith commitments of others..... it is unlikely that our listeners will detect that we are actually speaking about a God of love.

bear false witness against your neighbour" (Exodus 20:16). Christian witness can certainly involve constructive critique, but it should not involve "false witness".

In our multi-faith society there is also the potential to witness jointly, with people of other faiths, as people of faith. In our increasingly secular society, there is much to be gained by people of different faith traditions standing together to speak of ethical and spiritual values that benefit the individual and society. This can stand alongside the distinctive witness that each faith can also make.

> There is much to be gained by people of different faith traditions standing together to speak of ethical and spiritual values.

Ways forward

- ☐ **Offer to people of other faiths what you know and have experienced of Christ. But be ready to listen to others. By allowing time and space for questions, witnessing can be seen as journeying together.**

- ☐ **Learn about other faiths out of respect and sensitivity. Your willingness to learn is a mission statement about your vulnerability, your need for relationship with others and your desire to be enriched by the faith of others.**

- ☐ **Remember that witness to Jesus Christ is rarely effective through polemic or condemnation of the sincerely held religious beliefs of others, though it may happen through constructive critique.**

- ☐ **Be willing to co-operate with people of other faiths who seek, like you, for a better world.**

How far should we disagree with or challenge people of other faiths, if we have difficulties with what they believe and practise?

People involved in inter-faith dialogue sometimes appear to place greater importance on maintaining harmony and avoiding conflict than on tackling differences. In a world where religion is not innocent when it comes to conflict and violence, this can seem superficial, even two-faced.

People may say

- "Say it like it is! Differences between religions should be faced head-on. It's not just about samosas and tea. After all, the secular world is not afraid to question and even ridicule Christianity."

- "We should be cautious. It's always better to start with common ground, otherwise people get defensive."

- "We have to tell the truth. You can't dodge differences and difficulties. But raising them too early can be unhelpful. You have to be able to trust, and know that you are trusted, first."

To consider

Knowing when to raise potentially difficult questions is about getting the balance right between honesty and courtesy, and between honesty and caring. Courtesy and caring demand that trust and respect in a dialogue relationship should not be sacrificed by forceful criticism. Yet honesty demands that we should not avoid difficult questions that involve challenging or disagreeing with our partners in dialogue.

When and how these difficult questions should be raised depends on the context. In the past, some Christian missionaries condemned all other religions as false, in language that shocked and hurt the people who belonged to those religions. There are some Christians who do the same today. The people we are in dialogue with know this and can easily access negative material about their beliefs, written by Christians, on the internet. They can, therefore, be extremely sensitive to criticism. Where trust has been built up, however, what is difficult and perhaps painful can be raised.

Some of the most contentious questions are about social and ethical issues, where there may also be real differences among Christians. Willingness to raise such questions with people of other faiths should therefore be combined with a willingness to listen to the different views held by Christians.

Dialogue is a two-way process. People of other faiths may have difficulties with Christian doctrine and practice. If we ask difficult questions of others, we must be willing to have difficult questions asked of us. We need to know how to explain the hope and faith that lie within us.

> If we ask difficult questions of others, we must be willing to have difficult questions asked of us.

Ways forward

☐ Take care, when asking difficult questions, that your words do not come over as an attack on all that your partners in dialogue believe.

☐ Be prepared to listen and to have difficult questions directed at you also.

☐ Avoid raising the same questions at every meeting or in every context, even if disagreements persist. This could prevent any progress in mutual understanding.

Code of Conduct for Dialogue

The following is an extract from the Inter Faith Network Code of Conduct, adopted by the Methodist Conference in 1994. (See Appendix 1 for the complete Code of Conduct.)

When we talk about matters of faith with one another, we need to do so with sensitivity, honesty and straightforwardness. This means:

- **recognising that listening as well as speaking is necessary for a genuine conversation;**
- **being honest about our beliefs and religious allegiances;**
- **not misrepresenting or disparaging other people's beliefs and practices;**
- **correcting misunderstanding or misrepresentations not only of our own but also of other faiths whenever we come across them;**
- **being straightforward about our intentions;**
- **accepting that in formal inter faith meetings there is a particular responsibility to ensure that the religious commitment of all those who are present will be respected.**

Can we use our scriptures in inter-faith dialogue?

What attitudes do people of other faiths have towards the Bible? Is the Bible something that can be used as we speak to people of other faiths? Some Christians are unwilling to bring biblical passages or stories into their inter-faith conversations, fearing that they may do it insensitively or that the people they are speaking with might not show the same respect to the Bible as Christians do.

People may say

☐ "The Bible is the Word of God, a light to our path. It is my joy to share it with people of other faiths."

☐ "Where there is no respect for the Bible, I will not use it."

☐ "I've been enriched by reading the scriptures together with people of other faiths."

To consider

Using scriptures in inter-faith dialogue is an important way of sharing something precious of the Christian faith and learning about what is precious to other faiths. Many Christians find that sharing from the Bible, particularly some of the stories and parables that Jesus told, is a most effective way of communicating the essence of their faith. It offers others a way of understanding Christianity that is more accessible than talk about doctrine.

Sharing the Christian scriptures with people of other faiths also gives us the opportunity to hear another perspective on these scriptures, as we listen to the responses people make to them. We can learn from the example of Jesus when he asked his disciples, "Who do people say I am?" (Mark 8:27-33) – a question that shows Jesus placing value on the thoughts of people outside his immediate circle of disciples. When other

> The response of people of other faiths can offer us valuable insights into the Bible.

people identified Jesus with Elijah, John the Baptist or one of the other prophets, they were actually drawing on an element of Jesus' life and ministry that the disciples themselves did not recognise at the time: Jesus as the suffering servant. Similarly, the response of people of other faiths can offer us valuable insights into the Bible.

Christians can also find themselves enriched when people of other faiths respond to Bible passages by sharing from their scriptures. This can result in the discovery of remarkable convergences as well as differences. Similar stories may be present, but different interpretations placed on them. It is very important, though, to be sensitive to the fact that scriptures are used differently in different faith traditions. For example, many Christians are happy to discuss the historicity of biblical texts, but Muslims would not expect to discuss the Qur'an in this way. We should not force people of another faith to use methods they would not expect.

We should also remember that people of other faiths may find that the Bible does not resonate with them, or that certain sections do not. This can be a painful experience for Christians. For example, the challenges of apocalyptic texts such as Revelation, or texts that read exclusively such as John 14:6, may seem alien to people of some faiths. Relationships of trust and understanding are necessary if we are to discuss what these scriptures mean to us and listen without defensiveness to the responses of our partners in dialogue.

Ways forward

- [ ] **Find opportunities to use the Bible in inter-faith encounters. Be prepared to explain what biblical texts mean to you and to hear the response of others.**

- [ ] **Do not expect people of other faiths to accept biblical texts as authoritative, no matter how important they are for you.**

- [ ] **Take opportunities to hear and learn about the sacred texts of other faiths.**

How should we view and assess the scriptures of other faith traditions in comparison with ours?

Most world faiths have written texts that are considered holy, inspired, or revealed by God. This can pose a problem for Christians who believe that the Bible holds God's sole revealed message to the world. If the Bible is God's sole message, what status do other holy books have? If it is not, doesn't this somehow relativise the Bible?

People may say

☐ "I don't feel that I need any other scriptures; the Bible is God's truth and it is enough."

☐ "We can't judge the scriptures of other faiths if we don't read them."

☐ "Even if I did read other holy books, I could never read them like insiders do."

☐ "I've gained so much by opening myself to what is holy in other religions."

To consider

Scripture does not fulfil the same function in all faiths. The Old Testament of the Christian Bible is almost the same as the Jewish scriptures known as Tanakh. However, people from the two faiths interpret these scriptures differently: Christians in the light of the New Testament and their faith in Christ, Jews in the light of their continuing tradition and experience.

For Muslims, the Qur'an is the Word of God, every phrase a direct communication from God for the guidance of humans. The holiest body of sacred knowledge for Hindus is the Veda, the Sanskrit word for "knowledge". It is considered *shruti*, which means "that which is heard" or seen. The emphasis is, therefore, placed on the holy ancestors who heard, rather than the God who revealed. The word "eternal" rather than "revealed" is used for these Hindu scriptures. The holy book of the Sikhs is the Guru Granth Sahib. This is believed to be God's Word and the living presence of God among God's people. The canon of holy texts in Theravada Buddhism is a record of the teaching of the Buddha, the enlightened one; as a non-theistic religion, the idea of revelation does not enter.

These differences should be recognised and respected. Important to note also is that, just as in Christianity, differences can exist between members of the same faith about how their sacred texts should be used and interpreted. Yet none of this changes the basic issue here for many Christians: the status of the holy writings of other faiths.

There are no easy answers. Some of the points to consider elsewhere in this book stress that God does reveal God's self outside Christianity. If this is accepted, then surely God can inspire the holy texts of other faiths. The question then arises: if the holy texts of other faiths are inspired by God, what happens when they are placed alongside the Bible? Do they resonate with the Bible? Do they differ from it? Do they contradict it?

When the scriptures of different faiths are placed alongside each other, similarities, differences and contradictions can be discovered. The similarities occur particularly in ethical teaching, and in awareness of the love and grace of God. For example, it can be difficult to distinguish a Christian prayer to God from a Sikh, Hindu or Muslim prayer of devotion, when they are all placed side by side. Differences occur because the holy scriptures of the world's faiths arise out of different narrative traditions and different theological and doctrinal frameworks. They are to be expected, because the faiths of the world are different. Hardest of all to deal with are the contradictions, such as the affirmation of the crucifixion and resurrection of Jesus in the Bible and the denial that Jesus was crucified in the Qur'an.

> Similarities, differences and contradictions can be discovered.

A good way to work towards an answer to this question is to read some of the holy scriptures of other faiths, perhaps with people of that faith. In some parts of the country scriptural dialogue groups have taken place: for example, Jews and Christians reading the Hebrew Bible together (one text, different ways of reading); or Sikhs and Christians jointly reading the Guru Granth Sahib and the Bible. People who have taken part in such dialogue have often found that their own faith has been strengthened and illuminated by the witness of other sacred texts or by new readings of the Bible.

Ways forward

☐ **Expect to find the holy and wholesome in the sacred texts of other religions.**

☐ **Expect difference also, but do not use this to condemn the whole faith as false.**

☐ **Choose one faith other than Christianity and read some of the texts it considers sacred.**

Can Christians pray and worship together with people of other faiths?

This is a pressing question for people with friends in other faith traditions, especially at times of crisis. The need for inclusive public responses to national or international disasters or other events has sharpened the issue. How should church leaders approach public worship, or civic or national events, where representatives of many religions are present? At a local level, when formal worship by people of other faiths is not possible in Methodist churches, are there appropriate ways in which people of different faiths can come together to pray and worship?

People may say

☐ "No they can't. How can you pray or worship together when you can't even be sure you're worshipping the same God?"

☐ "Yes, they can, so long as you stress some common denominators and not differences."

☐ "Yes they can, and it really doesn't matter if prayers are quite different from each other because God can deal with all our inadequate words and poor insights; God will still be praised."

☐ "No, they can't. Even if they're praying together, they won't actually be praying *together*."

To consider

For all who believe in one God, it would seem to make sense to say that it is not only possible but desirable for people of different faiths to worship together. But it is not as easy as that. Monotheists of many faiths have difficulties with the idea of shared worship. For instance, for Jews and Muslims, the contested status of Jesus makes prayer or worship with Christians difficult. Some Christians are very happy to pray *for* people of other faiths, but would feel that they were losing integrity if they prayed *with* them.

> Monotheists of many faiths have difficulties with the idea of shared worship.

Does this mean, therefore, that worshipping together should be avoided completely? It does not. But distinctions must be made between different forms of inter-faith prayer and worship, and between different methods of enabling all present to participate. In the present, inter-faith prayer or worship is already happening in the following situations:

- pastoral situations, where a representative of one religion may be asked to pray with someone of another religion;
- civic services, for example on Holocaust Memorial Day or Commonwealth Day;
- shared times of prayer or worship within a local community, after a local, national or international tragedy;
- shared times of prayer within a local inter-faith group, where members have built up friendship and trust.

In these situations, different methods are used to enable people of all the faiths present to participate. In some cases, one member of each faith offers a reading or a prayer and those of other faiths observe with empathy, with no obligation to participate. In other cases, words or prayers are chosen that are considered to be inclusive, so that everyone present can share in them. In yet other cases, a shared time of silence is thought to be the best means of allowing each person to pray or meditate in his or her own way. It was the Roman Catholic Church that first made the helpful distinction between "praying together" and "coming together to pray". Silence is perhaps the best way to enable "coming together to pray" to happen.

Expecting people of different faiths to pray or worship together could be like asking teams of footballers, cricketers, table-tennis players and chess players to have a game of sport with one another – footballers with cricketers, table-tennis players with chess players. Sports people clearly have sport in common. But what they have in common cannot be reduced to a common activity, even if they might meet at a sports awards ceremony once a year. They simply cannot easily do together what they do separately, even whilst acknowledging the similarity, value and virtuosity of their separate endeavours. And yet their separate activities are clearly very similar.

If you think of it like that, pointing out the difficulty of sharing in prayer and worship with people of other religious traditions does not devalue the traditions but may be a proper way to respect them in their difference. Neither does pointing out the difficulty preclude all possibility of shared prayer and worship. Recognition of difference should not be coupled with a refusal to identify and work with what is held in common. In the case of traditions that hold to a belief in a God (or a Supreme Being or Reality) who is prayed to, exploration of what it might mean to share in prayer to such a God would seem an imperative. For Christians, belief in a God who is incarnate in the world underpins this imperative.

> Recognition of difference should not be coupled with a refusal to identify and work with what is held in common.

Ways forward

- [ ] **Remember that, in Christian understanding, all prayer and worship is response to God's initiative, and a way of participating in God's desires for, and action on behalf of, the world God created. This is a way of understanding what a person of another tradition is doing when they pray, even when (e.g. in Buddhism) God may not be named.**

- [ ] **Accept that religious traditions have very different ways of praying and worshipping, which cannot easily be reduced to a common practice.**

- [ ] **Be aware of opportunities to pray with people of other faiths. Respond to such opportunities within the integrity of your own beliefs and with sensitivity for the beliefs and feelings of others.**

Can there be true devotion to God in another religion?

Many Christians have been taught to see Christian devotion or worship as "true" devotion. Some, in recent decades, have observed the worship and devotional practices of people of other faiths and been deeply moved by the experience of the holy that has resulted. Others have observed and been perplexed. The questions that arise touch on how to make sense of what is experienced.

People may say

☐ "Of course there can. God can be worshipped in many ways and through many different routes."

☐ "Of course there can. But the best form of devotion can only occur in Christ."

☐ "No, there simply can't be true devotion to God in another religion."

☐ "Actually, I haven't the foggiest idea!"

To consider

The answer to this question must draw both on theological reflection and on experience. The "dialogue of religious experience" is now an accepted form of dialogue (see page 5). It was formally identified in 1984 by what is now the Vatican's Pontifical Council for Interreligious Dialogue. Visiting places of worship other than one's own, as a sympathetic observer, is recommended within this form of dialogue. It is, in fact, one of the best ways to get in touch with what shapes and inspires the life of another faith community. People who have done it often testify to the intense sense of the holy that they have encountered. On the basis of this, they have concluded that there must be true devotion to God in another religion.

Theological reflection supports this. If God the Spirit is at work in the world, and not just in the Church, then God will be seen at work in other religions. If God can reveal God's self wherever God chooses, then the activity of God in the devotion of religious traditions other than Christianity must be possible.

> If God the Spirit is at work in the world, and not just in the Church, then God will be seen at work in other religions.

This does not mean, however, that all devotion is inevitably "true devotion", in other words that the One God is automatically encountered through any devotional practice or through the exercise of any spiritual technique. This would not even apply to Christianity itself. Discernment is needed.

This section has concentrated on devotion as worship, but it is more than this. The challenge for Christians and others is to determine what "true devotion to God" amounts to in the whole of life, in spirituality, ethics and politics.

Ways forward

☐ Accept the challenge of defining what "true devotion to God" amounts to in Christianity.

☐ Ask people of other faiths what devotion to God means to them.

☐ Start from the assumption that a member of another religious tradition is truly devoted to God in belief and practice.

☐ Don't be afraid to engage in a dialogue of religious experience by visiting other places of worship.

Four types of dialogue or encounter

In 1984 the Roman Catholic Church identified four kinds of inter-faith dialogue or encounter:

- **dialogue of life – a living together in friendship;**
- **dialogue of joint social action – a working together for justice and peace;**
- **dialogue of the intellect – a coming together to seek clearer understandings of truth through discussion and debate;**
- **dialogue of religious experience – a sharing of insights from prayer and meditation.**

Can different faith communities work together?

There are now many settings where encounter between people of different faiths occurs, from our places of work to involvement in local voluntary organisations. In addition, the British government places importance on consultation with faith communities and seeks to encourage faiths to work together at a local level. For some Christians, this raises problems. Does working with people of other faiths, for instance, imply that we have to accept what they believe? And aren't the differences too great for a common purpose?

People may say

☐ "I've got some great friends of other faiths and we all think alike on local political matters. That's where inter-faith encounter should start."

☐ "Doing things together is confusing. In fact it's wrong because it implies that all religions are the same. Religions should keep to themselves."

☐ "I really like it when you see the imam, the rabbi, the Salvation Army captain and a couple of bishops at public and civic occasions. Whether or not faiths agree, they should take part."

☐ "We should get involved but should make clear where, as Christians, we do and don't agree with others."

To consider

It is easy to think in terms of "us and them" in our relationships with people of other faiths. Yet it need not be like this: people of different faith traditions do and, in some cases, must work together at local and national level. There are inter-faith groups and Councils of Faiths in many parts of Britain. Some meet to foster greater understanding between faiths, for example through discussing aspects of worship or belief. Others meet to co-operate on social and moral concerns, and service in the community. Others exist more formally to relate to local government structures or regional development bodies.

These are not clear-cut functions. One group may be involved in more than one type of activity. Broadly speaking, however, a division has developed between groups that stress *inter-faith* activity and those that stress *multi-faith* activity. Inter-faith activity means meeting together to enhance greater understanding between faiths. Multi-faith activity consists of working together on a common project such as urban regeneration; coming to know about the beliefs and practices of other faiths does not take first place.

Multi-faith activity has grown considerably since 2000, when the Local Government Act gave local authorities a statutory duty to prepare community strategies for promoting or improving "the economic, social and environmental well-being of their area…". Wide consultation was encouraged, especially with under-represented groups such as faith communities. The arrival of Local Strategic

Partnerships (LSPs) increased this trend. LSPs bring different parts of the public sector together with the private, community and voluntary sectors to work to ensure that public services meet the needs of local people. There is usually faith community representation on these. Community Empowerment Networks are also important: i.e. bodies that bring together community and voluntary sector organisations so that they can better link up with LSPs. Another tier is that of the Regional Development Authority. At all these levels, good relationships between different faiths are necessary to ensure that there is local input from all faiths.

In other contexts, people of different faith traditions find themselves working together in professional life and in voluntary work, when faith may prove important but not be the reason for working together. Health care, community and social work, and politics are three examples. In these situations, the challenge to all people of faith is to be prepared to make explicit where and how faith matters in public life, with agreements and disagreements openly acknowledged.

> The challenge to all people of faith is to be prepared to make explicit where and how faith matters in public life.

The Act of Commitment voiced in January 2000, at a meeting of nine faiths to mark the Millennium (see Appendix 2), indicates that there are many people in all faiths who seek to build a better and more humane society. If Christians do not co-operate with them in making their contribution, they may be losing a tremendous opportunity both to witness to their own faith and to contribute to public good. People of different faiths may have more public influence when they work together, even when differences remain.

Ways forward

☐ **Find out what forms of inter-faith and multi-faith co-operation already exist in your area.**

☐ **Talk to work colleagues or neighbours who you know to be of a different faith about the things that they consider important in public and political life. See if there are things you hold in common.**

☐ **Join a local community project. You may not know in advance whether people of another faith are involved. Even if they aren't, pay attention to what involvement teaches you about your own faith.**

What should we do if there is no response when we try to relate to other faiths in our neighbourhood?

Some churches and individual Christians have experienced rejection or a simple lack of interest when they have tried to establish links of friendship with another faith community in their neighbourhood. Such an experience can be hurtful and discouraging.

People may say

"Christians should wait, listen and keep the invitation open."

"Forget it! If you've tried once, that's enough."

"We should ask ourselves if we did anything that offended them; maybe we could have done things in another way."

"The Church should try harder; lack of interest may not mean hostility. Christians should not give up."

To consider

There is nothing in the Bible to suggest that we should offer courtesy, welcome or hospitality only when we expect a positive response. In Britain today, bridges of friendship need to be built between faith communities, if there is to be social harmony and social cohesion.

> Bridges of friendship need to be built between faith communities.

If a faith community rejects or ignores the hand of friendship, we should not immediately assume that it is not interested in building relationships. There are questions that should be asked: Are the members of the community still working hard to establish their sense of identity? Have they experienced discrimination and rejection from Christians in the past? Might they be experiencing religious discrimination in the present? Could some people fear that their children will leave their own faith, if they become too friendly with Christians? Has anything happened recently that might have caused mistrust of Christian motivations or a sense of threat from society in general? If the answer to any of these questions is yes, then this may explain the lack of response. The bombing of New York's twin towers in 2001, for instance, affected the attitude of some mosques towards other faiths, causing some to seek better inter-faith relations and some to withdraw from inter-faith activity.

People in another community may also not respond simply because they are over-stretched and under-resourced. At present, for them, inter-faith relations are not the top priority.

Another important question is whether there are clear lines of responsibility in the faith community concerned. Is there, for instance, one person who has responsibility for external relationships, so that requests for dialogue can be dealt with easily? If there is not, again this may explain a lack of response.

Ways forward

☐ **Don't be discouraged. Relations of mutual respect and trust can take a long time to build.**

☐ **Remember that a community has a right not to be forced into dialogue.**

☐ **Work through an inter-faith group or council, or through friendships made in the work place. These can sometimes bring better results than a direct approach to a place of worship.**

How should Christians respond to political parties that gain votes through exploiting religious differences?

There is evidence of increased support in some parts of Britain for political parties that present religious and cultural differences as a threat to Britain's identity. Such parties are often active in places characterised by poverty and unemployment, among white communities that feel excluded from the prosperity of Britain. The issue facing Christians is how such parties should be challenged.

People may say

- "Why shouldn't I support them? They're the only ones who understand what whites are feeling!"

- "We should do everything we can to expose their racist lies."

- "They're certainly dangerous, but aren't we giving them the oxygen of publicity if we draw attention to them?"

- "I don't like them, but, as long as there's poverty in Britain, they will keep on growing."

To consider

One method of extremist parties such as the British National Party (BNP) and the National Front is to exploit people's fears about religious diversity, whilst presenting themselves as champions of the Christian way of life. They have done this in several ways, from claiming that members of a particular faith are taking away jobs or funds from white communities to playing on religious symbols to present another faith, particularly Islam, as a threat to the identity of Christian Britain. One symbol used a few years ago was the Christian cross, the numbers 666 (the number of the "beast" in Revelation 13:18) written across it, with the words, "Islamic Britain – a cross to bear?" alongside. Much current literature emphasises the threat that asylum seekers pose to British culture and religion. Although religion may not be the primary focus, the message is often conveyed that the faith of asylum seekers increases the threat to Britain.

"Help us to win back Britain for the British" is one slogan these parties use. The meaning of this is sometimes masked. As one inter-faith officer in Lancashire has written of the BNP:

> It excludes anyone whose ancestors arrived in Britain after 1948. It does not include the Irish people who rebuilt the infrastructure of Britain after the Second World War. It does not include the Afro Caribbean people who came to work in our public services, transport and hospitals. It does not include the Indians and Pakistanis who were invited to work the night shift when the textile industry was in fact dying, or the Asians from East Africa who having built British colonies, found no place in them after independence. It does not include those who have come recently from India and the Philippines to nurse in our Lancashire hospitals.

The Britain of such parties is a white Britain. They bring in religion wherever they believe that they can gain electoral advantage by playing on religious as well as racial difference. The practical outcome

of their propaganda in some parts of northern Britain has been that people of faiths other than Christianity have been denied permission to establish a place of worship or a community centre – rights that should have been theirs as citizens of this country.

Racism like this is a denial of all that Christians in Britain should stand for. It is a denial of the oneness of all humanity under God. In 1994, eight principles for dialogue and evangelism were adopted by the Methodist Conference. The first of these is: "Our multi-cultural society is a gift from God, an expression of the sort of society God wants us to establish, within which all human beings can flourish." The same could be said of our religious diversity. It is a gift to Britain, which strengthens the religious and moral underpinning of our country. Britain is the richer because of its cultural and religious diversity.

> Britain is the richer because of its cultural and religious diversity.

It should be remembered that extremist parties appeal to three sorts of voter:

- those who live on the margins of our urban areas, where almost no one would live if they had the choice, places where the facilities are poor and the prospects for increased prosperity minimal;
- those who have little contact with people of other cultures and faiths and are as a result fearful that Britain is losing its identity;
- those who are racist.

In other words, extremist parties thrive not only because of overt racism in our society, but because of failures in our social and political system. They thrive because of poverty in our cities and a lack of social cohesion. They thrive because we do not know how our neighbours of other faiths and cultures live and what values underpin their lives.

Ways forward

☐ **Find out if any extremist parties are fielding candidates for election in your area or whether they are represented on your local council.**

☐ **Find out if Christians in your area, ecumenically or with people of other faiths, have made a statement or issued a leaflet pointing to the danger in voting for such parties; if not, press for this to happen.**

☐ **Find ways of standing in solidarity with people of other faiths if literature undermining them appears in your locality.**

☐ **Write to the press to give a Christian view of an inclusive society.**

But what will all this do to Christianity?

This question reveals a basic concern for many Christians. Christianity, some fear, will change out of all recognition if it mingles too much with other religions. It may not be able to maintain its grasp on "the hope that is within it" (adapting 1 Peter 3:15) and the insights we have been given through revelation.

People may say

☐ "It will change it beyond all recognition. Christianity will simply stop being Christian."

☐ "It will change it for the better. Christianity will be enriched. It will simply adapt and take on the best of what it finds around it, as it has always done."

☐ "It will change it. Other religions will change too, yet we'll all remain distinct."

☐ "It won't change, or at least not very much. How can it? Jesus Christ is the same yesterday, today and forever."

To consider

To think that Christianity is pure and will be tainted through contact with other faiths reflects a particular understanding of the relationship between Church and world. According to this view, Church is so detached from the world of which it is inevitably a part that Christians can remain untouched by their environment. Christians are in, but not of, the world (John 17:16; Romans 12:2). They are being shaped by God through prayer, worship, participation in a religious community and ethical living in keeping with their faith.

However, this detachment is never best understood as a complete separation (despite 2 Corinthians 6:17). The history of Christianity is a history of interactions with other worldviews and thought forms, which have brought change. The Church has never been static for long. The very integrity of Christianity has often been at stake, especially in the earliest Christian centuries when key understandings of Christian faith, such as incarnation and trinity, were first worked out. The fact that Christianity can be shown to have changed and

> The history of Christianity is a history of interactions with other worldviews and thought forms.

that Christians have often disagreed about the essence of the faith (for example, at the time of the European Reformations) shows that the claim to purity is problematic and far less easy to tie down than often supposed.

The way that the Christian faith has developed is interactive. The fact, though, that it still has a distinct identity shows that certain features have remained to make it recognisably Christian: belief in

the incarnation, for instance. Christianity's capacity to mutate and develop, whilst remaining identifiably itself, is clearly one of its strengths. It is also only what should be expected of an incarnational religion.

Each generation, therefore, has to think afresh about what it means to be Christian, to be followers of Christ. In the twenty-first century, this must take into account the multi-faith nature of British society.

Ways forward

- ☐ **Accept that Christianity will change in the future. It always has done.**

- ☐ **Accept that Christianity will also remain identifiably similar to what it has been before. This has always been the case.**

- ☐ **Trust God to guide the future of Christianity. Christianity does not need protection. Its only calling is to remain faithful to the revelation it has been given in and through Christ, by the Holy Spirit.**

The Inter Faith Network Code of Conduct, adopted by the Methodist Conference 1994

BUILDING GOOD RELATIONS WITH PEOPLE OF DIFFERENT FAITHS AND BELIEFS

In Britain today, people of many different faiths and beliefs live side by side. The opportunity lies before us to work together to build a society rooted in the values we treasure. But this society can only be built on a sure foundation of mutual respect, openness and trust. This means finding ways to live our lives of faith with integrity, and allowing others to do so too. Our different religious traditions offer us many resources for this and teach us the importance of good relationships characterised by honesty, compassion and generosity of spirit. The Inter Faith Network offers the following code of conduct for encouraging and strengthening these relationships.

As members of the human family, we should show each other respect and courtesy. In our dealings with people of other faiths and beliefs this means exercising good will and:

- respecting other people's freedom within the law to express their beliefs and convictions;
- learning to understand what others actually believe and value, and letting them express this in their own terms;
- respecting the convictions of others about food, dress and social etiquette and not behaving in ways which cause needless offence;
- recognising that all of us at times fall short of the ideals of our own traditions and never comparing our own ideals with other people's practices;
- working to prevent disagreement from leading to conflict;
- always seeking to avoid violence in our relationships.

When we talk about matters of faith with one another, we need to do so with sensitivity, honesty and straightforwardness. This means:

- recognising that listening as well as speaking is necessary for a genuine conversation;
- being honest about our beliefs and religious allegiances;
- not misrepresenting or disparaging other people's beliefs and practices;
- correcting misunderstanding or misrepresentations not only of our own but also of other faiths whenever we come across them;
- being straightforward about our intentions;
- accepting that in formal inter faith meetings there is a particular responsibility to ensure that the religious commitment of all those who are present will be respected.

All of us want others to understand and respect our views. Some people will also want to persuade others to join their faith. In a multi faith society where this is permitted, the attempt should always be characterised by self-restraint and a concern for the other's freedom and dignity. This means:

- respecting another person's expressed wish to be left alone;
- avoiding imposing ourselves and our views on individuals or communities who are in vulnerable situations in ways which exploit these;
- being sensitive and courteous;
- avoiding violent action or language, threats, manipulation, improper inducements, or the misuse of any kind of power;
- respecting the right of others to disagree with us.

Living and working together is not always easy. Religion harnesses deep emotions which can sometimes take destructive forms. Where this happens, we must draw on our faith to bring about reconciliation and understanding. The truest fruits of religion are healing and positive. We have a great deal to learn from one another which can enrich us without undermining our own identities. Together, listening and responding with openness and respect, we can move forward to work in ways that acknowledge genuine differences but build on shared hopes and values.

An Act of Commitment

The following "Act of Commitment" was said by representatives from nine faith communities at a Shared Act of Reflection and Commitment at the Palace of Westminster to mark the year 2000.

Faith community representatives:

> *In a world scarred by the evils of war, racism, injustice and poverty,*
> *we offer this joint Act of Commitment as we look to our shared future.*

All:
> *We commit ourselves,*
> *as people of many faiths,*
> *to work together*
> *for the common good,*
> *uniting to build a better society,*
> *grounded in values and ideals we share:*
>
> > *community,*
> > *personal integrity,*
> > *a sense of right and wrong,*
> > *learning, wisdom and love of truth,*
> > *care and compassion,*
> > *justice and peace,*
> > *respect for one another,*
> > *for the earth and its creatures.*
>
> *We commit ourselves,*
> *in a spirit of friendship and co-operation,*
> *to work together*
> *alongside all who share our values and ideals,*
> *to help bring about a better world*
> *now and for generations to come.*

Resources

Resources for Group Use

1. *The Life We Share: a study pack on inter faith relations*
   £10.00 plus £3.00 postage
   Available from: Methodist Publishing House, 4 John Wesley Road, Werrington,
   Peterborough PE4 6ZP
   or USPG, Partnership House, 157 Waterloo Road, London SE1 8XA

2. *Paths of Faith*, Elizabeth Harris (ed.)
   £8.00 plus £1.50 postage
   Available from: Christians Aware, 2 Saxby Street, Leicester LE2 0ND;
   www.christiansaware.co.uk

3. *Dialogue: A CMS study pack for use in small groups* (focuses on Christian-Muslim relations. Contains a video,
   My Muslim Neighbour, and material for four study sessions)
   £10.00
   Available from Church Mission Society, Partnership House, 157 Waterloo Road, London SE1 8UU;
   e-mail: info@cms-uk.org

4. Faith to Faith, a Christian agency that seeks to help Christians be effective witnesses to Christ in today's multi-
   faith society, offers courses and trainers on the following faiths: Islam, Sikhism, the New Age Movement,
   Buddhism. The study courses are written by Christian specialists.
   Information from: Faith to Faith, Carrs Lane Church Centre, Carrs Lane, Birmingham B4 7SX;
   e-mail: office@faithtofaith.org.uk

Journals

Of the journals that deal with inter-faith issues, one of the best is:

Interreligious Insight: a journal of dialogue and engagement
£24.00 per year for 4 issues
Subscriptions through the website: www.interreligiousinsight.org
Or send a cheque payable to "Interreligious Insight" to Interreligious Insight c/o World Congress of Faiths,
2 Market Street, Oxford OX1 3EF

Websites

The website of the Inter Faith Network for the United Kingdom has links to the websites of many of its member
faith communities: www.interfaith.org.uk

See also the website of the International Interfaith Centre in Oxford: www.interfaith-center.org

Courses

1. The United College of the Ascension in Birmingham offers short courses (1-3 days) on different aspects of inter-faith relations.
   Contact the college at Weoley Park Road, Selly Oak, Birmingham B29 6RD;
   e-mail: j.marks@bham.ac.uk

2. The London Inter Faith Centre offers a Certificate in Inter Faith Relations, suitable for those living in the London area who can travel to evening sessions.
   Contact: The London Inter Faith Centre, 125 Salusbury Road, London NW6 6RG;
   e-mail: info@londoninterfaith.org.uk

3. The Centre for Jewish-Christian Relations provides a number of educational programmes on the Jewish-Christian encounter. These include an MA, introductory 12-week courses and an annual 2-week summer school.
   Contact: CJCR, Wesley House, Jesus Lane, Cambridge CB5 8BJ;
   e-mail: enquiries@cjcr.cam.ac.uk; www.cjcr.cam.ac.uk

Further Reading on Inter-Faith Relations – a small selection

1. The scene in Britain:
   a. *Local Interfaith Activity in the UK: A Survey*, 2003, London, The Inter Faith Network for the United Kingdom
      This maps the patterns of local inter-faith activity across the UK.
      £8.95
      Available from: The Inter Faith Network for the United Kingdom, 8A Lower Grosvenor Place, London SW1W 0EN
   b. *Religions in the UK 2001-2003*, Paul Weller (ed.), the Multi-Faith Centre at the University of Derby and the Inter Faith Network for the United Kingdom, ISBN 0 901437 96 4 (this is the 3rd edition; it is hoped that a 4th will be possible)

2. Personal reflections on inter-faith relations:
   a. Ariarajah, Wesley S., 1999, *Not Without My Neighbour: Issues in Interfaith Relations*, Geneva, World Council of Churches
   b. Bishop, Peter, 1998, *Written on the Flyleaf: a Christian Faith in the Light of Other Faiths*, Peterborough, Epworth, £8.95
   c. Forward, Martin, 1995, *Ultimate Visions: Reflections on the Religions We Choose*, Oxford, Oneworld, £9.95
   d. Nesbitt, Eleanor, 2003, *Interfaith Pilgrims: Living Truths and Truthful Living*, London, Quaker Books, £8.00

3. Theological reflections on inter-faith relations:

a. Ariarajah, W., 1987, *The Bible and People of Other Faiths*, Geneva, World Council of Churches

b. Dupuis, Jaques, 2002, *Christianity and The Religions: From Confrontation to Dialogue*, Orbis Books & Darton Longman & Todd

c. Pinnock, Clark, 1992, *A Wideness in God's Mercy: the Finality of Jesus Christ in a World of Religions*, Zondervan

d. Sanders, John, 1994, *No Other Name: Can Only Christians Be Saved?*, SPCK

4. General books on inter-faith relations:

a. Forward, Martin, 2001, *Inter-religious Dialogue: A Short Introduction*, Oxford, Oneworld

b. Lochhead, David, 1988, *The Dialogical Imperative*, Maryknoll, New York, Orbis

5. Books on individual faiths:

a. Christians Aware produces a series of books to aid dialogue. Each one is beautifully illustrated and gives readers a chance to "meet" practitioners of the faith through their words:
Meeting Buddhists, Ramona Kauth & Elizabeth Harris (eds.) (forthcoming)
Meeting Hindus, Gwyneth Little (ed.) (£11.50 plus £3.00 postage)
Meeting Muslims (to be revised)
Meeting Sikhs, Joy Barrow (ed.) (£8.30 plus £1.70 postage)
Available from: Christians Aware, 2 Saxby Street, Leicester LE2 0ND
Enquiries: barbarabutler@christiansaware.co.uk

b. Several publishers offer short introductions to individual faiths. One of the best series is that offered by Oxford University Press (e.g. Kim Knott, 1998, *Hinduism: A Very Short Introduction*). Dunedin Academic Press (Edinburgh) is also preparing a series in *Understanding Faith* (see *Understanding Judaism* below).

c. Books written or recommended by practitioners of the faith concerned offer insights that cannot be gained through books written by Christians for Christians. The following are to be recommended:
Walpola, Sri Rahula, 1997, *What the Buddha Taught*, Oxford, Oneworld (a re-print of a classic)
Klostermaier, Klaus K., 2000, *Hinduism*, Oxford, Oneworld
Ahmad, Khurshid, 1999 (3rd Edition), *Islam: Its Meaning and Message*, Leicester, The Islamic Foundation
Rosen, Jeremy, 2003, *Understanding Judaism*, Edinburgh, Dunedin Press
Ajith Singh, Charanjit, 2001, *The Wisdom of Sikhism*, Oxford, Oneworld

Useful Addresses

1. The Inter Faith Network for the UK, 8A Lower Grosvenor Place, London SW1W 0EN
E-mail: ifnet@interfaith.org.uk

2. The Churches Commission on Inter Faith Relations, Church House, Great Smith Street, London SW1P 3NZ

3. The Churches Agency for Inter Faith Relations in Scotland, c/o ACTS, Scottish Churches House, Dunblane, Perthshire FR15 0JA

4. The International Interfaith Centre, 2 Market Street, Oxford OX1 3EF
E-mail: iic@interfaith-center.org

How *Faith Meeting Faith* came about

Faith Meeting Faith has been compiled by a working group drawn from the Methodist Church Inter Faith Relations Committee and the Methodist Church Faith and Order Committee. It responds to the task given to the Inter Faith Relations Committee, in co-operation with the Faith and Order Committee, by the Methodist Conference of 2001: to provide guidance for Methodist people and churches on the theology and practice of relationships with people and communities of other faiths. Although both Committees have been involved throughout in the production, final responsibility for *Faith Meeting Faith* lies with the Inter Faith Relations Committee.

Faith Meeting Faith builds on other documents adopted by the Methodist Church, particularly:

- *Principles for Dialogue and Evangelism: A Methodist Reflection on the Inter Faith Network's Code of Conduct* (1994 – the Code of Conduct, which was adopted together with the Principles, is re-printed in Appendix 1);

- *Called to Love and Praise* (1999) – a Conference Statement that affirmed the importance of building relationships with people of other faiths but recognised that a long process of discernment will be necessary on these issues.

Acknowledgements

The Methodist Church Inter Faith Relations Committee is grateful to the following people for their help in publishing this resource.

Dr Elizabeth Harris, Secretary for Inter Faith Relations, Methodist Church

Revd Canon Dr Michael Ipgrave, Secretary of the Churches' Commission on Inter Faith Relations

Professor Judith Lieu, Kings College, London

Dr Clive Marsh, Secretary of the Methodist Church Faith and Order Committee

Dr Helen Reid, Director of Faith to Faith

Revd Peter Russell, Chair of the Methodist Church Inter Faith Relations Committee

Revd Peter Sulston, Co-ordinating Secretary for Unity in Mission, Methodist Church

Ruth Nason, for her excellent editing, and the many groups and individuals, within Methodism and more widely, who so graciously gave their time to comment on the draft document

and the **Design and Production** team at Methodist Church House.